INSIGHT COM

GRan C

Compact Guide: Gran Canaria is the ideal quick-reference guide to this enchanting destination. It tells you all you need to know about the island's attractions, from its rugged mountain interior to its wonderful beaches, from its flower-filled villages to its lively capital, Las Palmas.

This is one of 133 Compact Guides, combining the interests and enthusiasms of two of the world's best-known information providers: Insight Guides, whose innovative titles have set the standard for visual travel guides since 1970, and Discovery Channel, the world's premier source of nonfiction television programming.

APA PUBLICATIONS
Part of the Langenscheidt Publishing Group

Insight Compact Guide: Grand Canaria

Written by: Hans-Peter Koch
English version edited by: Pam Barrett
Photography by: Gary John Norman and Gregory Wrona
Additional photography by: Mark Read, Pam Barrett 44/2
Cover picture by: Gary John Norman
Design: Roger Williams
Picture Editor: Hilary Genin
Maps: Polyglott/Maria Donnelly

Editorial Director: Brian Bell
Managing Editor: Tony Halliday

CONTACTING THE EDITORS: As every effort is made to provide accurate information in this publication, we would appreciate it if readers would call our attention to any errors and omissions by contacting:
Apa Publications, PO Box 7910, London SE1 1WE, England.
Fax: (44 20) 7403 0290
e-mail: insight@apaguide.co.uk

Information has been obtained from sources believed to be reliable, but its accuracy and completeness, and the opinions based thereon, are not guaranteed.

© 2003 APA Publications GmbH & Co. Verlag KG Singapore Branch, Singapore.

First Edition 1996, Second Edition 2002, updated 2003
Printed in Singapore by Insight Print Services (Pte) Ltd
Original edition © Polyglott-Verlag Dr Bolte KG, Munich

Worldwide distribution enquiries:
APA Publications GmbH & Co. Verlag KG (Singapore Branch)
38 Joo Koon Road, Singapore 628990
Tel: (65) 6865-1600, Fax: (65) 6861-6438

Distributed in the UK & Ireland by:
GeoCenter International Ltd
The Viables Centre, Harrow Way, Basingstoke,
Hampshire RG22 4BJ
Tel: (44 1256) 817987, Fax: (44 1256) 817988

Distributed in the United States by:
Langenscheidt Publishers, Inc.
46–35 54th Road, Maspeth, NY 11378
Tel: (1 718) 784-0055, Fax: (1 718) 784-0640

www.insightguides.com

GRan CanaRIa

◁ **Teror (p48)**
This village, a jewel of Canary Island architecture, is also the island's premier religious centre.

▷ **Mirador de Balcón (p87)** One of the most impressive views of the rocky West Coast is to be had from this point.

▷ **Las Palmas (p28)**
The island's lively capital is home to numerous buildings of considerable historical importance. In the Old Town, Vegueta, a UNESCO World Heritage Site, you will find the exquisitely restored Casa de Colón — an attractive museum that plays on its remote connection with Columbus.

◁ **Puerto Rico (p78)**
Upmarket Puerto Rico is family-friendly, and a centre for yacht racing and deep-sea fishing.

▷ **Cenobio de Valerón (p53)** A fascinating prehistoric site, these 300 tufa caves are a legacy of the island's original inhabitants, the Guanches.

△ **Maspalomas Sand Dunes (p74)** These spectacular mountains of sand are now a protected nature reserve.

◁ **Roque Nublo (p92)** The most dramatic of the rock monoliths that dominate the interior.

▷ **Dedo de Dios (p60)** The striking 'finger of God' pinnacle has become the symbol of the island.

▽ **South Coast Resorts (p71)** Ever popular, these resorts have something for everyone.

△ **Puerto de Mogán (p79)** This star resort aims to recreate the island's traditional ambience and architecture.

A Continent in Miniature

Gran Canaria, the focal point of the Canary Islands archipelago, is an island of great beauty, although this may not be immediately apparent when you're on the bus from the airport to Las Palmas. The landscape ranges from the endless sandy beaches of the south coast to the dramatic gorges and rock formations of the interior.

Beyond the resorts, there are sleepy fishing villages waiting to be discovered, historic town centres to admire, abandoned cave dwellings to marvel at and little squares for simply dozing under shady trees. Gran Canaria is both overcrowded and deserted: the visitor can get lost on a lonely beach or plunge into the nightlife of an international resort. While people bask in the sun at Playa del Inglés, snow can cap the peaks around Tejeda, barely 40km (25 miles) inland.

LOCATION AND SIZE

Gran Canaria is part of the Spanish autonomous region of the Canary Islands and is the third largest island in the archipelago (after Tenerife and Fuerteventura). The Canary Islands lie some 1,100km (700 miles) southwest of mainland Spain. They comprise the islands of Lanzarote, Fuerteventura and Gran Canaria to the east, and Tenerife, La Gomera, La Palma and El Hierro to the west. Gran Canaria lies some 63km (39 miles) from Tenerife and 197km (122 miles) from the African mainland, on a level with southern Morocco. The island is almost a perfect circle in shape and covers an area of 1,532sq km (592sq miles); its diameter at its widest point is 53.4km (33 miles). The highest mountain is the Pico de las Nieves (1,949m/6,394ft).

GEOLOGY AND LANDSCAPE

As recently as the 1960s, experts were still divided as to what caused this island to be formed some 16 million years ago. Today

Opposite: Maspalomas beach
Below: Ocean Park

it has been established that Gran Canaria is neither a broken-off segment of the African mainland, nor is it the remains of some sunken continent, but was formed by volcanic activity beneath the Atlantic Ocean. Continental drift made the ocean bed of the Atlantic particularly unstable in the region of the Canary Islands.

The oldest part of the island is what is now the west coast; the mountain massif in the centre, once a giant volcano, was formed later. Eventually there was no more molten rock to support the top of the volcano, and it fell in on itself, forming massive craters or calderas. The gorges *(barrancos)* radiating out from the centre of the island were formed by the subsequent process of erosion that took millions of years.

The vast stretches of sand on the south coast have nothing to do with the island's volcanic origins, but resulted from changes in sea level following the Ice Age. The white sand was washed ashore by the sea, the Maspalomas dunes being formed of nothing but the remains of crustaceans, ground to a fine powder over the millennia.

CLIMATE

Gran Canaria's climate is described as 'eternal spring'. Temperatures rarely rise above 26°C (79°F), except in July and August when they go

Below: coloured rocks at Fuente de los Azulejos
Bottom: Playa de las Canteras

somewhat higher. Furthermore, there is usually a gentle breeze, and the nightly minimum temperature rarely sinks below 15°C (59°F). Correspondingly, the water temperature seldom falls below 19°C (66°F), even in winter.

TRADE WINDS

These temperatures are a result of the north-east trade wind, a constant current of air which is warmed up over the equator and blows along the same route across the northern hemisphere every day of the year. Reaching the Canary Islands from a north-easterly direction and thus bringing cooler air, the wind is also responsible for bringing the clouds which pass across the low-lying islands of Lanzarote and Fuerteventura, but deposit their rain when they reach the higher central massif of Gran Canaria (1,900m/6,000ft).

The northern half of the island is frequently not only cloudy but also cooler than the rest. Above the favoured holiday resorts in the south the sun is rarely obscured by the trade-wind clouds. Temperatures here are thus appreciably higher.

This stable pattern dominates the weather of Gran Canaria for about 300 days of the year. Between November and January there may be short, heavy showers when an Atlantic trough forces the trade winds back, while a Sahara sandstorm may force its way across in the face of the trade winds during the summer months. When this happens, temperatures may soar for two or three days to around 40°C (104°F) while the warm *levante* wind whips sand from the Sahara across the island. The locals refer to this phenomenon as 'Africa weather' *(tiempo africano)*.

WHEN TO GO

The Canary Islands, especially Gran Canaria, are almost always in season. Central Europeans come in spring, autumn and winter, when it is cold at home, while the Spanish come in summer when the Iberian peninsula is too hot. Older people favour the climate because the low diurnal tem-

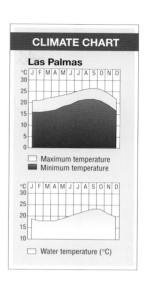

CLIMATE CHART

Las Palmas

☐ Maximum temperature
■ Minimum temperature

☐ Water temperature (°C)

El Puentillo on the north coast

Imported plants

None of the magnificent decorative plants, including hibiscus, bougainvillaea, oleander, begonia, the bird of paradise flower and a variety of acacias and poinsettias, which are lovingly nurtured in Gran Canaria's parks and gardens, are native to the island. They have all been imported at some time or another from distant tropical or subtropical countries. Thanks to the climate, however, they are invariably healthier and bigger than the equivalent northern European specimens. What may be cultivated as a house plant in England will be a large and splendid bush on Gran Canaria.

perature range (annual average 7°C/13°F) places no strain on the heart and circulatory system. The *levante*, however, can be troublesome for those suffering from respiratory problems. If you wish to avoid this you should not go to Gran Canaria during July and August. The prospect of rain should not dissuade anyone from visiting the archipelago in winter. Even during November and January, the wettest months, there is rarely more than 30mm (1.2 in) of rain on the coast.

The most popular time to visit Gran Canaria is the week before Easter and the Easter period itself, as well as the Spanish holiday months of July and August and the period between Christmas and the New Year. If you want relative peace and quiet and with the weather at its best, you are recommended to visit during May, June and October. These are also the months during which the hotels offer the most favourable terms.

FLORA

As can be expected of a 'miniature continent', as Gran Canaria is often called, the vegetation is extremely varied, ranging from Canary pine trees, in the higher central areas, to the palms and exotic fruit trees such as mangos, pawpaws and avocados in the south.

In the hot, dry zone, below 400m (1,300ft), local plants have developed a variety of survival methods. In order to minimise loss of moisture through transpiration, many plants have narrow leaves, or have developed a hard wooden exterior. Others transform their moisture into a thick sap. Succulents of the euphorbia family contain a white milky sap which is a strong irritant.

Prickly pear

TYPICAL SPECIES

Typical species to be found in the arid zone are *Cardón cardonales*, or pillar euphorbia (commonly known as the candelabra cactus), which abounds in the south of the island, reaching tremendous heights. The *tabaiba* is a common shrub with narrow leaves, resembling a miniature tree. The other cactus-like plant commonly found on the hillsides and bordering the road towards the north and centre of the island is the prickly pear *(Opuntia ficus indica)*, which was brought to the Canaries from Mexico in the 16th century. For many years it became an essential part of the island's economy. The plants were used to cultivate the cochineal, an insect whose larvae produce a red dye and was traded in huge quantities during the late 18th and early 19th centuries, before man-made dyes made an appearance. There has recently been an upturn in demand for cochineal, and new prickly pear plantations have been created, particularly on Lanzarote.

DRAGON TREES AND DATE PALMS

The distinctive dragon tree *(Dracena draco)* is closely related to the yucca. It is commonly found in the central upper regions of the island. The dragon tree, with its dark green sword-shaped leaves, formed an essential part of the original inhabitants' religious beliefs and was a vital ingredient in their medicinal remedies.

The Canary date palm *(Phoenix canariensis)* is a close relative of the date palm of North Africa and the Arab countries, but has larger, more luxuriant leaves. Mostly found in the south, it bears a small date-like fruit known as the *tamara*, which

Below: papaya
Bottom: abundant flora

is, in fact, inedible. It is interesting to watch the pruners at work, as they scale the rough trunk with the aid of a leather sling to 'shave the beards' of the emblematic trees, which appear on the coat-of-arms of Las Palmas de Gran Canaria.

PINE FORESTS

Below: pine forest, looking across to Tenerife
Bottom: landscape in the centre of the island

Found in the mountainous interior, the Canary pine *(Pinus canariensis)* might be less majestic than its Nordic counterparts, but it thrives particularly well on these arid, volcanic islands. Because its resinous wood is totally fire-proof, it invariably survives the not-infrequent forest fires. It is not unusual to see whole areas where the trunks of the trees stand in a charred wilderness, while up on high the green needles glisten in the sunlight. These needles, which are almost 30cm (12in) long and grow in clusters of three, are adapted to extract the maximum amount of water from the air, made moist by the clouds borne by the trade winds.

Native species forming the undergrowth in the pine forests include the *Amagantes*, a pink-flowering rock rose, and *Codeso*, a leguminous plant which bears bright yellow blossoms in spring. Native to the mountainous interior is the imposing Canary *Tajinaste*, which can grow up to 2 metres (6ft) high.

LUSH LAUREL

Of the lush forests which covered the island before the Spanish conquest, only a few square miles, or about one percent, of the original woodland remains in the north. This is the home of the Canary laurel tree *(Laurus canariensis)*, which grows in the cloud layer created by the trade winds and whose leaves are used for culinary purposes. One of the finest laurel forests is Los Tilos de Moya *(see page 53)*.

FAUNA

Although the flora of the Tertiary eras has survived on the islands, visitors will be pleased to know that much of the fauna has not. One of the most delightful things about the archipelago in general is that there are no dangerous animals to be encountered anywhere, either on land or in the sea. The most common creature on Gran Canaria is the lizard *(lagarto)*, which can often be spotted dashing from bush to bush. This endearing planteater should not be confused with the smaller geckos *(peringué)*, which live on mosquitoes and may even find their way into hotel bedrooms.

There are a number of birds of prey (sparrowhawk, kestrel, buzzard and African vulture), and some colourful species such as the hoopoe.

Visitors to the south of the island may be treated to the nocturnal perambulations of the cockroaches, especially if there are gardens and bougainvillaea nearby. Walking barefoot in the dark is not advised.

SAFE SEAS

The sea is clear of danger, though sometimes visitors on the beach at Las Canteras may encounter nasty-looking jellyfish (known locally as *aguavivas*), which do have a nasty sting. In the rocky areas of the south coast, watch out for the *erizo del mar*, the sea urchin or 'sea hedgehog' which, as its name suggests, is very prickly. But there are no sharks to worry about, and whales and dolphins are rarely sighted.

> **Canaries**
> The 18th-century Spanish naturalist and historian José de Viera y Clavijo believed the islands' name came from *cantare*, the Latin verb 'to sing', because the conquerors had been so impressed by the sweet song of the indigenous birds. Some people find the canary birds *(Serinus canarius)* something of a disappointment: although they sing as exquisitely as their domesticated counterpart, their greyish-green plumage is much less conspicuous. They belong to the finch family and only gained their bright plumage after they had been caged.

Below: Serinus canarius
Bottom: fun on the beach

ENVIRONMENTAL ISSUES

Tourism, particularly of the sun-sea-and-sand variety, is always hard on an environment, and Gran Canaria's is no exception. However, the economic need to diversify in tourism, while responding to environmental criticism, is likely to produce a 'greener' future for the island. In recent years much has been done to ensure that the pristine quality of the seawater is maintained, mainly by exploring the possibilities of recycling waste waters and solids, while industries are endorsing energy-conscious programmes to improve their environmental image.

Below: the reservoir, Barranco de Aldea
Bottom: wind power at Agaete

SUN AND WIND POWER

To anyone from colder climes, it must always have seemed a mystery that solar energy was not widely used on Gran Canaria, where there was no shortage of sunshine. Now, particularly in the south of the island, much has been done to rectify this, with installation of solar facilities.

Wind power has also experienced an upturn in popularity as an alternative way of producing electricity. Developments such as the windmill field at Pozo Izquierdo may not be as decorative or scenically beautiful as Don Quixote's windmills on La Mancha, in Cervantes' novel, but they are highly efficient.

PROTECTIVE MEASURES

New government bills on energy production and use and protection of the coastline have gone a long way to ensuring that environmental issues feature high on everyone's agenda. Many areas of the island have been designated natural parks and special nature reserves, which precludes the possibility of land speculation and destruction. In fact, over 40 percent of the territory on Gran Canaria is protected to some degree.

A rural park, the largest on the island, encompasses the region around Cruz de Tejeda and Roque Nublo; a protected reserve covers 4,000 ha (8,880 acres) around Inagua in the west; and the Tamadaba pine forest, near Agaete, has been designated a nature park.

Environmental protection groups – Gran Canaria's ASCAN is the largest in Spain – are becoming more active and influential. Tourism-related companies have assumed responsibility for financing parks and reforestation projects; and town councils are adopting more environmentally-conscious approaches in planning schemes.

RESTRICTED ACCESS

Some of the remaining natural wonders of Gran Canaria are inaccessible to visitors and islanders alike. The laurel forest of Los Tilos de Moya *(see page 53)* has been closed to the public in order to prevent further damage. The *turismo rural* initiative is encouraging ecologically-sound tourism *(see page 19)* and the newly-traced *caminos reales* (royal paths), which follow the routes of ancient tracks, are now the only ways that walkers are allowed to reach some of the more remote parts of the island.

POPULATION AND RELIGION

Around 760,000 of the 1.7 million inhabitants of the Canary Islands live on Gran Canaria – some 364,000 of them in the capital, Las Palmas. Although Gran Canaria is only the third-largest island in the archipelago, it is the most densely

Water

The Canary Islands suffer from a shortage of fresh water, worsened by increased consumption during recent decades. Early explorers confirm that the island was once green and water was plentiful. The dense forests that covered Gran Canaria were destroyed to make way for water-intensive farming crops – sugar cane, bananas and tomatoes – which greatly reduced the capacity of the soil to store water.

The lowering of the water table exacerbates the problem, as sea water seeps into the porous volcanic rock, making wells and watercourses brackish. The growing number of tourists places increasing demands on water supplies, but farming still accounts for more than half the island's total water requirements.

Until recently, water was a private industry, but in the south it is now run by a franchise called Elétrica Maspalomas SA, who supply 13 million cubic metres of water a year, much of which comes from desalinated sea water. Waste water in the southern resorts is used to irrigate parks, gardens and golf courses.

Religious souvenirs

inhabited. The busy port and the tourism industry have attracted numerous people from other parts of the world who have set up permanent residence on the island.

The people of Gran Canaria, more than those of the other Canary Islands, have a highly cosmopolitan outlook. And, like most people who live in isolated regions, they are community-minded. Above all, they stress that they are *canarios* first and foremost, not Spaniards.

From the time of the Spanish conquest, until the end of Franco's dictatorship in 1975, Roman Catholicism was the only official religion. As in other parts of today's more tolerant Spain, there are now communities of Anglicans, Baptists, Mormons, Muslims and Jehovah's Witnesses.

Below: Teror resident
Bottom: Las Palmas harbour

LANGUAGE

The official language on Gran Canaria is Spanish *(Castellano)*. However, a strong local dialect is widely spoken; its main characteristics are the swallowing of final consonants, the increased use of the subjunctive, the pronunciation of 'z' as 's', as in South America, rather than a lisped 'th' as in most of Spain; and the adoption of some Latin American vocabulary – for example, '*patata*' (potato) becomes '*papa*'.

The islanders also use words of their own: a bus is a '*guagua*', pronounced 'gwa-gwa'; and a few words have been borrowed from the English traders and sailors who were once so familiar in the port. A Canarian knife is a '*naife*' and a cake is a '*queque*'. English and German are widely understood and spoken in tourist centres.

ECONOMY

Because of its distance from the mainland, the Canary archipelago has always enjoyed special status within the Spanish state. When the import and export trade was set up by British entrepreneurs, the islands were awarded the status of duty-free ports. Even after full integration with the EU in 1995, Gran Canaria remained a free-trade zone, and the regional government, keen to attract new investment, wants it to stay that way.

Whatever eventually happens in this regard, the geographical isolation of the archipelago means that it qualifies to be treated as a peripheral area within the EU, which entitles it to various subsidies and aid programmes.

A LINK WITH THE WORLD

For a long time, Las Palmas' port, the Puerto de la Luz, was the island's only link with the outside world. Through here passed trade, emigrants and incomers. In the 1880s, its development as a harbour for steamships was largely responsible for the revival of Las Palmas, and a boost in its bid for supremacy over Santa Cruz de Tenerife.

Much of Gran Canaria's economic activity is still closely linked to the port. As part of a vast modernisation project, the harbour moles have been extended, a reorganisation that has also led to a major facelift being carried out on the Parque Santa Catalina; this is where the British merchants, Elder and Miller, erected the first export/import warehouses and offices – one of which now houses a science and technology museum, the Museo Elder *(see page 42)*. This is usually the first area to be explored by many of the cruise parties which stop off at Las Palmas.

Entrepreneurs
Thomas Miller (1805–85) was the first of the great English entrepreneurs to change the face of the Canary Islands *(see page 41)*. It was his son, James (1839–1915), who, at the request of the island authorities, shipped from England the great bronze dogs that still stand guard in the Plaza de Santa Ana in Las Palmas.

Boats of Sardina

TOURISM

Gran Canaria's principal source of direct and indirect employment comes from the service sector, of which tourism is a major part. Most tourism is located in the south of the island, while most of the islanders live in the north.

In recent years substantial EU funds have been put to good use in enlarging and strengthening the island infrastructure – roads, airports, hospital facilities, desalination plants and the like – necessary to support a massive influx of visitors (around 3½ million a year according to the most recent available figures).

The main nerve centre of tourism is on the southern stretch of coast between San Agustín and Puerto de Mogán, specifically in the Playa del Inglés and Maspalomas area. This is sun, sea, sand and sangria tourism, and is mostly geared to visitors on package-holidays, whose agencies block-book many of the large hotels and apartments.

ALTERNATIVE TRENDS

However, a lot of EU money has been ploughed into rural options to the north – luxury cave dwellings to hire for a romantic weekend, farmhouses to rent for self-catering holidays, and rural hotels, some of which offer activity programmes, from language courses to hiking and transcen-

Below: Puerto Rico marina
Bottom: sun on the seafront

dental meditation, are all part of the *turismo rural* initiative. There is also a rising interest in conference visitors, especially in and around Las Palmas. A new motorway network is under construction – parts are already open – which will take traffic around rather than through Las Palmas and relieve the chronic traffic congestion.

With a firm and long-standing tradition of quality tourism since the 1960s, Gran Canaria is now shaping up in preparation for new trends in international tourism. Greater emphasis is being laid on the desirability of resurrecting the island's cultural heritage, such as the various festivals and celebrations, and in rediscovering the pre-Hispanic history of the islands, in an attempt to show how distinct the roots of the Canary Islanders are from those of mainland Spaniards.

AGRICULTURE

Sugar cane, the first agricultural export of an island with no natural resources, was introduced by the Spanish early in the 16th century and exported after processing. However, competition from the cheaper sugar of Central America meant production began to decline before the century's end. Grapes were subsequently cultivated, and the Canary Malvasía (Malmsey) wine was sold all over Europe, although Gran Canaria was less suited to viniculture than Tenerife, and had only a small share of this trade.

BANANAS

During the 19th century cochineal was a major branch of the economy *(see page 11)*, but its importance declined with the advent of aniline dyes. Bananas were introduced from Indochina and subsequently marketed by the British in the 19th century. But the heyday of banana growing came to an end during World War I, and although it continued to form an important part of the economy for decades, it has now seriously declined.

The quality and taste of the Canary Island banana is more than a match for its Central Amer-

> ### Purple dye
> Along with cochineal *(see page 11)*, another less commercially important dye was produced on the island. This was the purple one that came from the orchilla weed, and which has a long history on the Canaries. The Romans, who prized purple, wrote of the Purpuriae islands where they found this substance – although there is some dispute over whether they meant the Canaries or the island of Madeira.

Below: sugar press, Ingenio
Bottom: banana plantation, Arucas

ican counterpart, but its small size means that it is almost unsaleable in the European market. In addition, production costs are much higher than in other countries. It takes 400 litres (88 gallons) of irrigation water on Gran Canaria to harvest 1kg (2.2lbs) of bananas. In tropical Costa Rica, on the other hand, no irrigation is necessary at all, and wages are also considerably lower.

Until the end of 1995, a market for the bananas was guaranteed by Spain. Since then, subsidies for continued cultivation have been made available by the European Union, but this has not halted the decline and local farmers have been forced to diversify into exotic vegetables, cut flowers, pot plants and the like.

Below: onion picker
Bottom: tomato plantations,
San Nicolás de Tolentino

TOMATO CULTIVATION DECLINES

Gran Canaria is the Canary Islands' largest producer of tomatoes for the European market. Their cultivation is centred largely around San Nicolás de Tolentino in the west of the island. However, the tomato is suffering a similar fate to that of the banana. Thanks to their low labour costs, countries such as Morocco have made dramatic inroads into the Canary Islands' markets – including those within the EU. It is not unusual to see piles of tomatoes being dumped by their disgruntled farmers as a protest against European rulings, quotas and lack of protectionism.

ADAPTING TO THE EU

There are large contingents of foreigners on the island, working in various capacities. Until the beginning of the 1990s, the largest group was Korean, due to the marked dominance of the Korean fishing fleet in Puerto de la Luz. But port conditions and EU restrictions on fishing have resulted in the exodus of this fleet and created severe hardship in this sector of the economy.

Despite all these problems, not all is doom and gloom. The transition to forming part of the EU has been relatively untraumatic for the Canary Islands. Perhaps the ease with which the islanders have adapted to the new circumstances is hardly surprising. After all, they have only had a degree of autonomy for a relatively short while and are used to adopting policies imposed from the outside by a central government in Madrid.

INDUSTRY

Industry is gradually getting stronger in Gran Canaria. Obviously, the distance from markets and high transport costs have been weighty factors in dissuading industry from establishing itself on the islands. However, the collaboration of the university (formed by popular demand in 1990) with industry, above all in the fields of energy production, bodes favourably for the future. Fish farming and the commercial development of seaweed derivatives are two of the successful joint ventures undertaken to date.

POLITICS AND ADMINISTRATION

Each of the Canary Islands forms an administrative unit, while the archipelago is divided into two provinces, which together combine to form an autonomous region, established in 1982.

The *Cabildo Insular* is the administrative body on each island and is responsible for all decisions above town or village level. It deals, for example,

Below: Puerto de la Luz, Las Palmas and (bottom) a view of the city's port

In recent years there has been a movement towards rediscovering cultural roots. Many inhabitants of Gran Canaria claim to be directly descended from the Guanches. In Gáldar, which still styles itself the Ciudad de los Guanartemes (City of Rulers), many of the streets have indigenous names and local people will say that 'people in this town have Guanche blood in the veins'.

A book was recently published containing Guanche names, and an increasing number of babies are being called Tamara or Tanausu.

with questions of road construction and environmental protection.

Las Palmas is the capital of the province of the same name, to which the islands of Lanzarote and Fuerteventura also belong. The second province, based in Santa Cruz de Tenerife, covers the other four islands. The seat of regional government alternates every four years between Las Palmas and Santa Cruz, a compromise in the rivalry for supremacy between the two capitals.

PROTECTING CANARIAN INTERESTS

In the late 19th century a small but vigorous independence party, influenced by the Latin American countries that had gained freedom from Spain, was formed in the Canary Islands, but little came of it. During the 20th-century years of dictatorship, all calls for independence were stifled. A short-lived campaign of separatist violence followed Franco's death in 1975, but the voice of moderation prevailed.

The moderate right-wing party ATI (Asociación Tinerfeña Independiente) was formed, with demands that the Canaries' special status should be recognised; it was particularly successful in local elections. The Coalición Canaria was formed in 1993 and is now one of the three main parties on the islands, after the conservative PP (Partido Popular) and the social democratic PSOE. It is a colourful coalition of communists, left- and right-wing nationalists and separatists, all united in order to protect Canarian interests.

Guanche skull, Museo Canario, Las Palmas

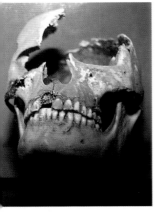

THE GUANCHES

The original islanders are known as Guanches. The name originated on Tenerife and means 'sons of the earth'; it is now used as the general term for all the indigenous people of the islands. The Guanches mummified their dead and buried them in caves. The mummies so far discovered – and the scant remaining written evidence – have led scientists to place the original islanders' ethnic origins in north-west Africa.

Language, political organisation and culture varied from island to island. On Gran Canaria, there was an hereditary monarchy and an aristocracy into which citizens could be elected. The leader of the noblemen was the Fayan, who combined the role of chief judge and high priest.

DAILY LIFE

The Guanches did not have the wheel, nor did they use bows and arrows, and there is no firm evidence that they could sail. They mostly lived in groups of caves, in which an entire village could be housed. Only when space became limited did they build stone houses, whose design can be deduced from the natural stone dwellings that are still in use all over the Canary Islands.

They lived on wild fruits and berries. There was no game, so pigs, sheep, goats and dogs provided not only meat but also the materials for covers and clothes. Fish formed a part of their diet, as did dates, mushrooms and roots. The national dish, *gofio*, was originally prepared from fern roots.

What became of the Guanches? Those who were not butchered or sold into slavery mixed with the colonisers, inter-married and were converted to the Christian religion. It was all a long time ago, but the islanders have not forgotten that they had a culture before the Spanish arrived.

Below: keeping order in Las Palmas
Bottom: local school children

HISTORICAL HIGHLIGHTS

c 3000BC Settlement starts on Canary Islands. Finds suggest that the earliest inhabitants are Cro-Magnon people who could have come from the African mainland. They are later followed by at least one more wave of settlers, probably from the Mediterranean area.

From 1200BC Regular visits by the Phoenicians and later the Carthaginians, but no trading contacts are established with the original inhabitants.

25BC According to an account written by Pliny the Elder, King Juba II of Numidia and Mauritania, appointed by Rome, orders an exploration of the Canaries. Remains of buildings, but no people, are discovered on the eastern islands of Lanzarote and Fuerteventura.

AD150 The Greek geographer Ptolemy shows the islands on his map of the world. The map shows the westernmost edge of the world (his prime meridian) running through the western tip of the island of El Hierro.

1312 The eastern Canary Islands are accidentally rediscovered by a Genoese of Provençal origin named Lanzarote Malocello, when his ship is driven off course on a journey to England. He spends almost 20 years on the island that is later named after him.

1341 Boccaccio mentions four Canarian slaves, goatskins, tallow, red-dyed wood and red earth brought back by the Genoese steersman Niccoloso da Recco. This visit is followed by several plundering expeditions by Genoese, Catalan, Majorcan and Basque seafarers.

1344 Luís de la Cerda, scion of the Spanish House of Castile, is appointed king of the Canary Islands by Pope Clement VI. He never sets foot on the islands.

1391 Thirteen monks sent to the Canary Islands to spread Christianity are murdered. This is followed by a bloody campaign of revenge against the local population, after which the survivors are imprisoned and enslaved.

1402–6 Robert of Bracamonte, presented with the still-independent Canary Islands by Henry III of Castile, hands them on to his French cousin, Jean de Béthencourt. The latter claims the islands of Lanzarote, Fuerteventura, El Hierro and later La Gomera on behalf of Spain, but fails in his attempt to take Gran Canaria.

1477–83 A Spanish force led by Juan Rejón lands on Gran Canaria. The island is ruled by two chiefs, Tenesor Semidan in the west and Doramas in the east. In 1478, the Spanish found the town of Las Palmas and embark on their conquest. Tenesor Semidan eventually converts and sides with the Spaniards, but many of the native inhabitants pursue a bitter struggle against the invaders. They are finally subdued by the forces of Pedro de Vera and Alonso Fernández de Lugo.

1480 Under the terms of the Treaty of Toledo, Portugal's claim to the Canary Islands is finally abandoned.

1492 Christopher Columbus briefly stops on the island of La Gomera, then diverts to Las Palmas for ship repairs, before he sails on to the west and discovers America.

1494–6 After suffering initial defeat at Matanza de Acentejo, Alonso Fernández de Lugo succeeds after three more campaigns in wresting Tenerife from the Guanches, who have been weakened by a plague epidemic. In the decades that follow, the Canary Islands gradually become an indispensable sea base for trips to America.

c 1500 Sugar cane forms the first monoculture and the first agricultural product. Merchants from Seville make vast profits; the heaviest work is undertaken by slaves brought from Africa and Las Palmas becomes a slave market. From 1554, the sugar-cane industry declines as a result of competition from the West Indies and Brazil.

From 1543 The capture of the fortress of La Isleta, originally built to protect Las Palmas, marks the beginning of a series of pirate raids over the next 200 years. French, British, Dutch and Berber fleets sail between the islands. Las Palmas is the subject of the most severe attack when it is stormed by the forces of Pieter van der Does, a Dutch buccaneer.

1700–1950 Poverty forces numerous Canary Islanders to emigrate. Cuba and Venezuela are favoured destinations.

1830 A short economic boom follows the introduction of the cochineal, an insect whose larvae produce a valuable red dye. The prosperity is brought to an end by the invention of aniline dyes.

1852 Isabella II declares the Canary Islands a free-trade zone.

1890 The British introduce bananas as a monoculture on the archipelago.

1911 Limited self-administration councils – *cabildos insulares* – are allowed on the islands. Gran Canaria hosts its own assembly.

1927 The Canary Islands are divided into two provinces. Santa Cruz de Tenerife becomes the capital of the western province, and Las Palmas de Gran Canaria capital of the eastern province.

1936 On July 18 Francisco Bahamonde Franco, the military governor of the Canary Islands, initiates the three-year Spanish Civil War from his base in Tenerife. Three days later the islands are in the hands of the Fascists.

1956 The first charter plane lands on Gran Canaria. Tourism rapidly developes into the most important industry. In 1974 the airport at Gando is opened.

1978–82 Following the death of Franco (in 1975) and the restoration of the monarchy, the new Spanish constitution joins the two Canary Islands provinces to form the Autonomous Region of the Canary Islands, now one of 17 such autonomous regions of Spain.

1986 Spain joins the European Union and negotiates a special status for the Canary Islands.

1995 The Canary Islands are fully integrated into the European Union but retain some important tax privileges.

1996 In the national elections, the Coalición Canaria, formed in 1993, wins 24 percent of the vote in Las Palmas province (26 percent in Tenerife), thereby taking four seats in the national parliament in Madrid. The regional government is keen to preserve the islands' status as a Free Trade Zone.

2000 Latest available figures show that more than 3. 5 million people a year visit Gran Canaria.

2002 The euro becomes the currency of Spain and the Canary Islands.

2003 In May, the Partido Popular makes electoral gains in Gran Canaria.

Map
on page
31

*Preceding pages: Puerto
de las Nieves
Below: popular pastime in
Parque Santa Catalina
Bottom: under the palm trees,
outside Bar Las Ranas*

1: Las Palmas

Capital city, port, trading centre, metropolis, garden city, shopping mecca: Las Palmas de Gran Canaria has something of everything. There are six-lane urban motorways and narrow streets in which the traffic builds up into jams. High-rise developments overlook the town from the surrounding mountains. Elegant department stores, ancient covered markets and street traders' stalls recall those of Rio or Cannes, while the bay of Las Canteras is one of the largest natural swimming pools in the world. The best way to discover the many faces of Las Palmas is on foot. You should allow two full days to explore the city's mixture of modernity and ancient history.

HISTORY

The town's history begins on the very day Gran Canaria was conquered. Juan Rejón landed in June 1477 in the bay which was later to become the Puerto de la Luz harbour. Rejón and his troops marched off in a southerly direction. It is said that he met an elderly Guanche woman, who recommended that he pitch camp on a river meadow *(vegueta)* in a grove of palm trees *(las palmas)*. The invading army established its headquarters in this very place, beneath shady fruit trees and

with a flowing river, the Guiniguada, to supply fresh water all the year round. According to legend, the old woman appeared to Juan Rejón in a dream as St Ana. For this reason, the cathedral of Las Palmas is dedicated to Ana, who became the city's patron saint.

THE CITY TODAY

The old quarter of Vegueta has remained the heart of the city, and it is from this point that Las Palmas spreads out in a northerly direction. Today the historic centre of Vegueta is a protected area, and in 1990 it was declared a UNESCO World Heritage Site.

The city derives its income largely from service industries; indeed, almost 80 percent of the population makes its living in this way. However, tourism, which was initially centred on the island capital, moved its centre of activity in the 1970s to the south coast *(see page 69)*. Some hotels closed down and the buildings were put to new uses as council housing or administrative offices.

PRIESTS, PIRATES AND SLAVES

These changing economic fortunes have repeatedly cast a shadow across the town's history. Las Palmas became a cathedral city in 1485 and in 1504 the seat of the Inquisition. During its first golden age as the trading centre for sugar cane and African slaves, British and Dutch pirate ships cruised off the coast in order to capture fleets from America or at least to plunder the city's riches. Sir Francis Drake and John Hawkins were both defeated at sea, as was the Dutch buccaneer Pieter van der Does, who nonetheless managed to raze the city to its foundations in 1599.

The fertile neighbouring islands of La Palma, La Gomera and Tenerife soon overshadowed Gran Canaria and its capital. When Napoleon occupied the Spanish mainland and deposed the king, La Laguna on Tenerife declared itself the capital of the islands. Las Palmas experienced a brief boom in 1881, when Fernando León y

Island rivalry
There has always been rivalry between Las Palmas and Santa Cruz de Tenerife, and the founding of the Autonomous Region of the Canary Islands in 1982 did not end it. Today, the seat of island government alternates every four years between them. And yet Las Palmas, by virtue of its population, its port and the longer history, still claims to be the capital of the Canary Islands.

Hotel Santa Catalina façade

Castillo, a native of Gran Canaria, was nominated foreign minister of Spain. He ordered the development of the port in his home town; the chief engineer was his brother, Juan.

THE OLD TOWN

The maze of narrow streets of the Old Town of ★★★ **Vegueta** nestles on the west side of the Fuente de Mendoza and Calvo Sotelo motorways. History is omnipresent here. At every turn you will see carved wooden balconies, Moorish decorative elements on the doorways, and even Ionic columns in front of the stately buildings. Tucked in between are *palacios* which look like fortresses, with patios full of brightly coloured flowers.

Going to the top
A sleek and swift modern lift to the right of the cathedral's main entrance will take you most of the way up the tower. A short flight of steps then leads you to one of the cupolas, from where there is a great view over the city.

Below: Catedral de Santa Ana
Bottom: statue in the Plaza

THE CATHEDRAL

Dominating the scene is the ★★ **Catedral de Santa Ana ❶** (open Mon–Fri 10am–4.30pm, Sat 10am–1.30pm; access only through Diocesan Museum; admission charge). Situated at the eastern end of Plaza de Santa Ana, its twin towers overshadow the Old Town. Construction work on the triple-naved building started not long after the Spanish arrived in 1497, but it took almost 400 years to complete, which explains the variety of architectural styles to be spotted both inside and out: Gothic in the interior at the back of the building and in the chapels along the left aisle, baroque in the San Fernando chapel, Renaissance in the right aisle, and an eclectic mixture in the crossing cupola. The neoclassicist elements on the facade, like many of the statues inside the cathedral, are the work of the Canary Island sculptor José Luján Pérez (1756–1815).

THE MUSEO DE ARTE SACRO

The **Museo Diocesano de Arte Sacro** (open as above; entrance in Calle Espíritu Santo) is set around a lovely cloister called the Patio de los Naranjos (Patio of the Orange Trees). It houses church treasures and religious paintings as well as booty from former Spanish colonies, including a number of notable Aztec works of art. There is also an impressive modern series of *Stations of the Cross* by local artist, Jesús Arencibia.

Star Attractions
● **Vegueta**
● **Catedral de Santa Ana**

PLAZA DE SANTA ANA

In front of the cathedral is the Old Town's main square, the ★ **Plaza de Santa Ana**, for more than

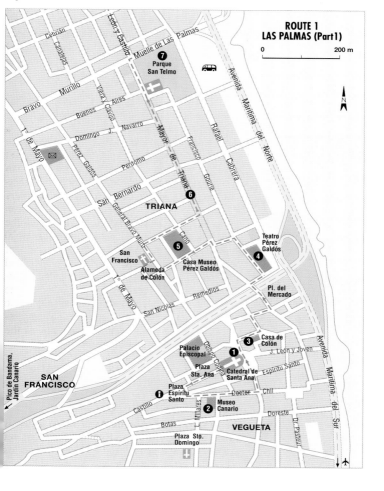

**ROUTE 1
LAS PALMAS (Part 1)**

0   200 m

N

Cebrián

Canalejas

Muelle de Las Palmas

❼
**Parque
San Telmo**

Avenida Maritima del Norte

Murillo

Vieira y Clavijo

Aires

Bravo

Buenos

Navarro

León y Castillo

Mayor de Triana

Francisco Gourié

Rafael Cabrera

de Mayo

Domingo J.

Pérez Galdós

Perdomo

San Bernardo

San General Bravo Muro

❻

TRIANA

Cano

**Teatro
Pérez
Galdós**

❺

**San
Francisco**

**Casa Museo
Pérez Galdós**

❹

**Alameda
de Colón**

Remedios

**Pl. del
Mercado**

de Mayo

San Nicolás

**SAN
FRANCISCO**

◄ Pico de Bandama,
Jardín Canario

**Palacio
Episcopal**

Obispo Codina

❸ **Casa de
Colón**

J. León y Joven

❶

Espíritu Santo

**Plaza
Sta. Ana**

**Catedral de
Santa Ana**

Avenida Maritima del Sur

ℹ
**Plaza
Espíritu
Santo**

Doctor Chil

Castillo

Millares

❷ **Museo
Canario**

Doreste

Botas

VEGUETA

Dr. Pasteur

**Plaza Sto.
Domingo**

✈

Map on page 31

500 years the most important square in Las Palmas. The square is bordered by magnificent palaces built for the church dignitaries.

One is the **Palacio Regental**, which is largely 17th-century, although the façade dates from 1867. The Canarian balcony is older, as is the huge and splendid doorway, which survived a fire that destroyed the town in 1599, following the invasion of Dutch buccaneer Pieter van der Does. Above it are the coat of arms of the kingdoms of León and Castile.

Little remains now of the adjoining **Palacio Episcopal** (Bishop's Palace) except a single-storey façade, giving a hint of former splendour.

Crushed carpets

In mid-June the Plaza de Santa Ana is the hub of the Corpus Christi celebrations (dates vary), a time of religious processions and secular enjoyment. The square is covered with a magnificent, patterned carpet of flowers which is walked on, filling the air with the scent of crushed petals.

ISLAND GOVERNMENT

Huge bronze statues of dogs, the island's heraldic animals, stand guard outside the cathedral; and at the other end of the square is the building housing the **Casas Consistoriales** (Offices of Island Government). Although over 150 years old, this is still the newest building in the plaza. The original structure was reduced to ashes on Easter Sunday 1842, after the roof truss was hit by a rocket. The Easter holiday is still marked by letting off fireworks in the plaza. At present the building is undergoing substantial renovation work – but not because of firework damage.

Below: pre-Hispanic pot, Museo Canario
Bottom: Casa de Colón

MUSEO CANARIO

On Calle Dr Verneau, not far from the plaza, is the ★★★ **Museo Canario** ❷ (open Mon–Fri 10am–8pm, Sat–Sun 10am–2pm; library Mon–Fri 10am–8pm; admission charge). This is the finest museum in the archipelago.

It houses the Canary Islands' largest and most comprehensive collection of objects dating from pre-Hispanic times, and will fascinate visitors who are interested in the early history of the islanders. The pottery, tools, mummies and skeletons of the original inhabitants are presented in a series of informative displays. The museum also contains a comprehensive collection of Cro-Magnon skulls, lined up row upon row in glass cases. Also on view is a replica of the Cueva Pintada in Gáldar *(see page 54)*.

CASA DE COLON

Another place that should be included on every visitor's itinerary is ★★ **Casa de Colón** ❸ (open Mon–Fri 9am–7pm, Sat–Sun 9am–3pm; free). Colón is the Spanish name for Christopher Columbus and it is claimed, with very little supporting evidence, that he stayed here when it was the home of the first island governor.

Be that as it may, the museum is well worth a visit. The colonial-style building was restored in the early 1960s, but the richly decorated doorway, the well in an inner courtyard and parts of the stonework date from the time of the Spanish conquest. The rest of the complex comprises houses built over the last three centuries. This was, incidentally, the birthplace of operatic tenor Alfredo Kraus, in 1927.

The voyages of discovery are presented with great clarity by means of model ships, a replica of the cabin of *La Niña*, one of Columbus' fleet, maps and nautical equipment. There is also a splendid collection of paintings on long loan from Madrid's Prado museum, a collection of pre-Columbian artefacts discovered on the Ecuadorian island of La Tolita, Peruvian carpets, and two noisy parrots in the courtyard.

Star Attractions
● **Museo Canario**
● **Casa de Colón**

Below: Casa de Colón window
Bottom: street kiosk

Map on page 31

Man of letters

Galdós was known as the 'Spanish Balzac'. He wrote more than 100 novels and many plays, and is one of the most widely read Spanish authors to this day. He was a social critic, a republican and an anticlerical. Recognition on the international literary scene helped him to achieve a breakthrough in conservative Spain. He became a republican senator in Madrid in 1910, and was elected to the same role when he returned to Las Palmas in old age, in 1914.

TRIANA

The **Triana** district adjoins Vegueta. Named after 16th-century Andalusian settlers and bearing the same name as one of the old quarters of Seville, it is the oldest shopping and commercial district in Las Palmas. To reach it you must cross a busy, traffic-filled dual carriageway. There is no underpass but there are plenty of traffic lights to make the crossing easier. Adjoining the Vegueta and Triana districts, lie Arenales and Lugo, two quarters which visitors are advised to ignore.

TEATRO PEREZ GALDOS

On the other side of the main road dividing the two quarters stands the **Teatro Pérez Galdós** ❹ (currently closed for renovation), named after the Canary Islands' most famous son, the best-known Spanish novelist of his time, Benito Pérez Galdós (1843–1920). Opened in 1919, the theatre was designed by Miguel Martín-Fernández de la Torre and decorated by his distinguished brother, the Modernist artist, Néstor *(see page 38)*. Outside stands a statue of French composer, Camille Saint-Saëns (1835–1921), who spent some happy times in Las Palmas.

Pérez Galdós

GALDOS'S BIRTHPLACE

A short distance on, in Calle Cano, the house where Galdós was born and spent his early years is now the ★★ **Casa-Museo Pérez Galdós** ❺ (open Mon–Fri 9am–7pm; sometimes open Sat–Sun; guided visits on the hour; free). The building is a fine example of Canary Island architecture, with a picturesque courtyard. It houses the most comprehensive collection of writings by and about Galdós, and is furnished with items from his houses in Madrid and Santander, many of them, like some of the paintings on the walls, the work of Galdós himself. In the study, a life-size wax model of the writer sits at the desk.

The guided tours are conducted in Spanish only, but they are worth taking, even if you don't understand very much of the language, in order to enjoy the house and its contents.

PLAZOLETA DE CAIRASCO

If you crossed the main road a little further up, on a level with the cathedral, you would come to the attractive little **Plazoleta de Cairasco**. The Hotel Madrid, one of the city's oldest hotels, has tables out under the trees along the right-hand side of the square. At the far end stands the imposing **Gabinete Literario**, a Modernist building splendid enough to have been declared a 'Monumento Histórico Artistico'. Once a theatre, it is now home to a literary society and therefore private, but lunch or a drink in the adjoining restaurant allows you to admire the interior and to sit in comfort on a shady terrace.

ALAMEDA DE COLON

To the left of the little plaza is an elongated square called the **Alameda de Colón**. A bust of Columbus surveys the scene. At the south end of the square, La Caja de las Canarias, a savings bank that does a great deal for the arts, funds exhibitions, films, music and theatre performances in a cultural centre (CICCA) housed in an imposing building with stone-framed doorways.

Star Attraction
● Casa-Museo Pérez Galdós

Below: Gabinete Literario
Bottom: the Plaza de las Ranas

Maps on pages 31 & 40

Below: Calle Mayor de Triana
Bottom: Parque Doramas

At the north end of the square is the pretty, colonial-style **Iglesia de San Francisco**. Destroyed in the fire of 1599, it was rebuilt during the 17th century, and there are later additions. The original wooden *mudéjar*-style ceiling was retained, and the exquisite Moorish decoration can still be admired, although the church is only occasionally open. Much revered is the Virgen de la Soledad, a madonna said to be a look-alike of the church's founder, Isabella I.

CALLE MAYOR DE TRIANA

The Triana district is almost as old as Vegueta, but has a much more bustling atmosphere. Crossing it is the **Calle Mayor de Triana** ❻, a granite-paved street that is closed to traffic. This pedestrian precinct, with its art nouveau façades, is not only one of the most fashionable shopping areas in Las Palmas, but also a popular street where older residents stroll or stop to talk and young people congregate in groups.

There is a variety of stores specialising in all kinds of goods, from small electrical shops to fashionable shoe shops, jewellers and a branch of Marks & Spencer. Some particularly noteworthy façades are **No 35** and **No 80**, both dating from the second half of the 19th century. There are also several attractive façades showing the influence

of Modernism (the Spanish version of art nouveau) in the neighbouring streets (Domingo J. Navarro and Buenos Aires). Don't miss the Librería Archipélago on Calle Travieso, which has a wide choice of books on the Canary Islands.

PARQUE SAN TELMO

Calle Mayor de Triana leads to the **Parque San Telmo ❼**, where the subterranean central bus station, the **Estación de Guaguas**, is located (with small shops and telephone cabins alongside it). This is many people's introduction to Las Palmas, as buses from the airport and from the southern resorts arrive here.

There's a pretty little chapel, the **Ermita de San Telmo**, dedicated to the patron saint of fishermen, with a fine coffered ceiling in *mudéjar* style. Under shady palms and *fisco* trees, visitors sit and refresh themselves with drinks from a lovely Modernist kiosk, decorated with gleaming tiles.

CITY OASES

If you are getting hot and tired you can get one of several buses from here to the next point of interest; some routes follow the Avenida Marítima, the busy carriageway parallel to the sea, passing the Fuente Luminosa, a fountain that is lit up at night. Otherwise, walk along Calle León y Castillo. On a level with the the **Muelle Deportivo** (yacht harbour) and the swimming pools of the **Club de Natación Metropol**, you will reach the **Ciudad Jardín**, an attractive district of villas and gardens, dating from the 1920s.

Here, too, is the ★ **Parque Doramas ❽**, a flower-filled and palm-shaded garden named after a Guanche chief who resisted the invading Spaniards, until the bitter end *(see box)*.

GRAND HOTEL

This urban oasis is dominated by the luxurious **Hotel Santa Catalina**. Founded in 1890 by the British entrepreneur, Alfred L. Jones, and built by

> **Death of a leader**
> According to legend, the powerful Guanche chief, Doramas, was pierced by the lance of Pedro de Vera, the first Spanish military governor, in 1480 while fighting him in single-handed combat on Montaña de Arucas *(see page 51)*. The Guanche warriors, deprived of their leader, refused to surrender and threw themselves into the *barranco* (ravine). The monument at the entrance to the Parque Doramas recalls this desperate act.

Guanche memorial, Parque Doramas

Map on page 40

Miguel Martín-Fernández de la Torre, it is the oldest five-star hotel on the island and still the best address in town. Visitors may like to stop for a cooling drink on the verandah before continuing their tour. To the northwest of the hotel lies another large swimming pool, **Club de Natación Julio Navarro**, and to the south lie the Pueblo Canario and the Museo Néstor.

PUEBLO CANARIO

Built in mock Canary-Island style, the ★ **Pueblo Canario ❾** or Canary Village, was established in 1939 by Miguel Martín-Fernández de la Torre, based on an idea of his artist brother, Néstor. The village was planned exclusively for tourists – which made it quite innovative for its time. It is an attractive complex of restaurants and handicraft shops (selling everything from embroidered table cloths to Canary knives) as well as a helpful tourist information office.

Folkloric performances
In the Pueblo Canario on Sunday at 11.30am there are displays of folk music and dancing by performers in traditional dress. It is worth going along just to see the fantastic costumes, quite apart from the beautiful and melancholy songs. Entry to these performances, which last about an hour, is free.

MUSEO NESTOR

In honour of the artist, one of the houses has been turned into the ★★ **Museo Néstor ❿** (open Tues–Sat 10am–8pm, Sun 10.30am–2.30pm; admission charge). Néstor Martín-Fernández de la Torre (1887–1938), always known simply as

Pueblo Canario

Star Attraction
● **Museo Néstor**

Néstor, was the first Canary Islands artist to achieve international recognition. He is regarded as one of the leading representatives of Modernism, and carried out a large number of projects in this style in mainland Spain – where he spent much of his life – as well as on his native island. In Las Palmas he was responsible for the decoration of the Teatro Pérez Galdós *(see page 34)*.

As well as a collection of furniture and designs for stage settings, the museum contains a permanent exhibition of Néstor's most famous paintings. Among his favourite themes in later life were the countryside of his native island and the plants and animals to be found there. This he immortalised in a series of pictures called *Visiones de Gran Canaria.*

Néstor's most important works are the picture cycles, *Poema del Mar* and *Poema de la Tierra*, with recurring themes of earth, people, animals and the waves of the Atlantic.

SHOPPING CENTRES

Bordering this miniature garden city is the shopping district of **Alcaravaneras**. Keep walking (or take one of the frequent buses) along León y Castillo and you will come in due course to the broad **Avenida Mesa y López**, which runs from the port to the Plaza de España. Branches of Spain's best-known department store, El Corte Inglés, can be found on both sides of the street, alongside international fashion outlets, exclusive boutiques and perfumeries, discount jeans shops and optical and electronic goods stores.

Exotic fruits, silvery fish, crisp salads and piles of gleaming vegetables will be found just round the corner (Calle Galicia) in the covered market, the bustling **Mercado Central ⓫** (open Mon–Sat 8am–2pm).

SANTA CATALINA DISTRICT

We have now arrived at the very heart of Las Palmas. Here, where the sea forces the town onto a narrow causeway of land, lies the ⋆**Santa**

Museo Néstor

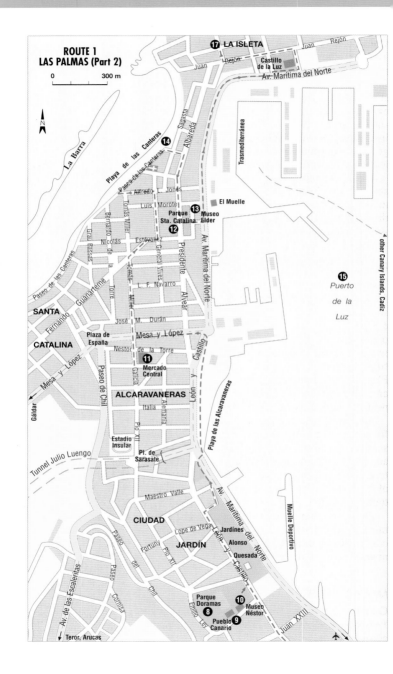

Catalina District and the park of the same name. This is a main tourist area and yet another shopping centre. The blend is fascinating: junk shops full of dusty souvenirs from all over the world stand cheek by jowl with others stocked with expensive jewels and furs. There are bazaars stacked high with goods in disorderly profusion, in which you will find high-quality electrical goods at competitive prices. In between are countless bars and cafés.

Sailors from the nearby port stroll through the streets, as African traders ply their wares, trying to tempt tourists making their way into town from the nearby hotels. Nowhere else in Las Palmas is there such a cosmopolitan atmosphere as here.

PARQUE SANTA CATALINA

The narrow streets lead straight up towards the ★★ **Parque Santa Catalina** ⑫, the liveliest square in town. At all hours of the day or night, everyone gathers here, be they early birds or night owls. Businessmen come in the morning to swallow a quick *cafecito* instead of breakfast, tourists from the hotels bordering the nearby beach, the Playa de las Canteras, arrive on sightseeing trips and at lunchtime you will see workers from nearby offices grabbing a quick bite of tapas.

After lunch, elegantly dressed ladies stop here for coffee, and in the evening young couples and sailors from the port take over. In among them all are street hawkers and multilingual waiters, lottery ticket vendors, shoeshine boys, and groups of men playing draughts and chess – and, unfortunately, the odd pickpocket, so be careful.

The park is not really a proper park at all, but rather a spacious plaza with a few areas of green, colourful splashes made by flower beds, and a number of outdoor cafés.

MUSEO ELDER

On the port side of the park is the smart new ★★ **Museo Elder** ⑬ (open Tues–Sun 10am–8pm; admission charge; entrance from the marina side

Map opposite

Star Attraction
● Parque Santa Catalina

Tartanas
Among the other attractions of Parque Santa Catalina are the horse-drawn carriages called *tartanas* which wait here to be hired. They'll take you for a leisurely drive through the city. It's difficult to avoid the traffic, but a pleasant way to see the sights while resting your feet.

Parque Santa Catalina

Map on page 40

👁 **English entrepreneurs**
The Museo Elder is housed in a converted, and much extended, warehouse that belonged to the 19th-century British trading company of Miller and Elder. These entrepreneurs were among those responsible for building the Muelle Santa Catalina, the first jetty in the new port. Previously, ships had been loaded and unloaded offshore, a risky business in bad weather.

James Miller also set up Las Palmas' first electricity company. His father, Thomas, who became wealthy exporting cochineal, is honoured with a street named after him, running parallel to the port.

Museo Elder

of the building).This is a splendid science and technology museum, with plenty to interest even the unscientifically minded. It's wonderful for hot, bored children, too, as there are numerous inter-active exhibits, a space station, an industrial robot spot-welding a car, and even an incubator where those with sufficient patience can watch chicks hatching from eggs.

PLAYA DE LAS CANTERAS

From Santa Catalina it is just a short walk to the Paseo de las Canteras, the beach front promenade and the broad sweep of golden sands that forms the ★ **Playa de las Canteras** ⑭. The remarkable feature of this beach is **La Barra**, The Barrier, which lies a few hundred metres offshore in the warm waters of the Atlantic – the ocean is still clean at this point. The reef is 2.5km (1½ miles) long and transforms the sea into a vast natural lagoon – the largest swimming pool in the world, as it is often called. Surfers, with or without surfboards, enjoy the southern end of the beach, where the waves roll unbroken onto the sand.

The Playa de las Canteras is a refuge for local people at weekends, in the early evenings and in their long lunch breaks. It is also very popular with mainland Spanish holiday-makers. The wide strip of beach is dotted with deckchairs, pedalos and every type of water sports equipment for hire. Local boys play football, in areas where they are not warned away from sunbathers; groups gather for impromptu games of bingo. Lifeguards watch over the scene, making it an ideal beach for families with small children.

RESTAURANTS AND RELAXATION

Side by side along the seafront stand elegant hotels and apartment complexes, some of which have seen better days. The traffic-free promenade is 5km (3 miles) long and serves as a buffer between the bustle of town and the beach idyll. Its numerous little oases of palm trees provide space for bars and cafés, discotheques and restaurants. From fishermen's taverns to Chinese or gourmet Italian, there is somewhere to suit every taste. You will even find a German beer cellar and an Austrian coffee-house, as well as two of the city's most popular restaurants, El Cerdo Que Ríe and El Gallo Rojo *(see page 109)*.

North African street traders, dignified and striking in their flowing robes, set up stalls along the promenade, where they sell jewellery, pottery and basketware.

Star Attraction
● **Museo Elder**

Music by the Sea

At the southern end of the beach, the stark outline of the **Auditorio Alfredo Kraus** seems to rise from the sea. The tenor was born in Las Palmas, in the Casa Colón. The impressive auditorium named after him is home to the city's Philharmonic Orchestra and is the venue for concerts by musicians from all over the world. Close by stand the Palacio de Congresos (Conference Centre), a large bronze statue of Kraus and the giant Las Arenas shopping centre – although not visible from the beach.

Castillo de la Luz

It will not take you long to cross the peninsula, at its northern, narrowest point. Continuing along

Below and bottom: views of Playa de las Canteras

Map on page 40

the noisy Avenida Marítima del Norte you will come to the **Castillo de la Luz** . Built during the 16th century, as can be recognised from the Gothic framework surrounding the doorway, the fort once served to defend the town and harbour from marauding pirates, who posed a threat to life and trade.

The Castle of Light is currently being renovated; when finished, it will house a museum and arts centre. In the afternoon, local people like to play *boules* in the little park surrounding the fort.

ISLETA

Below: Puerto de la Luz
Bottom: El Muelle

If you want to enjoy the panoramic view from Las Coloradas, the highest point of **La Isleta ⓑ** you may prefer to take a taxi or bus No 41 (which starts at Parque Sanata Catalina). The highest peak (239m/784ft) is visible from afar on the northern edge of town. From the top of a bare hill, under a tall wooden cross, you will have a majestic view of the town, harbour and ocean.

HARBOUR OF LIGHT

The eastern side of the peninsula follows the port, but it's a noisy, traffic-filled stretch. Best get a bus to the Muelle de Santa Catalina (the port side of the park), where a bright blue and yellow shop-

ping and entertainment complex, **El Muelle**, opened in 2003, overlooks the water. Close by, under an awning like a ship's sail, is a new bus station, built underground.

From El Muelle you can appreciate the vast size of the **Puerto de la Luz ⓰**, the Harbour of Light. It was created at the end of the 19th century as a major job-creation project, masterminded by a local engineer, Juan León y Castillo, whose brother, Fernando, was a minister in the Spanish government. Today it is the largest port in Spain, but it is struggling to retain its supremacy, as a number of African ports compete for its position as the turntable for sea traffic between three continents – Europe, Africa and America.

The harbour of Las Palmas is still important as a tourist port as it serves as the hub for the main ferry links between the islands of the archipelago. South of the working port lies the Club Náutico; the Playa de Alcaravaneras, a beach frequented mostly by local families; and the **Muelle Deportivo**, from where yachtsmen set out to cross the Atlantic. Las Palmas is the final port for taking on supplies before the long haul westwards. Frequent visitors in winter are the stylish yachts en route to the Caribbean. A new promenade, with shops and cafés, has been built beside the yachting harbour, which makes a pleasant place to walk, away from the traffic fumes.

CHANGING FORTUNES

The Harbour of Light is losing a number of its former essential functions. The cruise ships of the Cunard Line have long since ceased to tie up at the Muelle Reina Sofía, heading instead for the port of Los Mármoles on Lanzarote. Las Palmas fishing fleet is still the largest in Spain, but Moroccan fishermen can fish the Sahara Bank much more cheaply than their Canarian colleagues.

This in turn affects the fish processing industries. During the 1930s there were 27 factories; today only one survives. And recently, the Korean fishing fleets, which used Puerto de la Luz as their Atlantic base, have pulled out.

> **Leisure and luxury**
> In its heyday as a leisure port the Puerto de la Luz was a glamorous place. The *Queen Mary* and the *Queen Elizabeth*, and later the *QE2*, called here, as did the luxury Royal Mail ships to South Africa, all disembarking wealthy and well-known passengers for a tour of the city before they went on their way. Between 1967 and 1971, when the Suez Canal was closed, the ships of the P&O line also stopped here. The golden age came to an end in 1973, when the oil crisis hit and the price of fuel soared.

Castillo de la Luz

Map
on page
40

The era of Las Palmas as a naval base is coming to an end. The end of the Cold War meant that an Atlantic headquarters for the Spanish Admiralty was no longer of vital importance. But despite the decline, the port is still extremely important. This is partly due to its strategic geographic location, and partly because the port area of Las Palmas, together with the industrial area at Arinaga – form a Free Trade Zone. Companies operating within the zone are exempt from tax and customs duties, which helps to promote the growth of the regional economy, and increase international trade. Hence the large volume of container traffic passing through the port – around 380,000 containers annually.

Below: frangipani in the
Jardín Canario
Bottom: view of Las Palmas

JARDÍN CANARIO

After the beach and sightseeing routine of Las Palmas, the combination of peace and fresh air, together with the rich variety of the island's botanical species, are good reasons to visit the ★★ **Jardín Canario** (open daily 9am–6pm; free). This botanical garden lies in the hamlet of La Calzada near Tafira Alta, an elegant suburb 8km (5 miles) southwest of Las Palmas.

If you are driving, follow the road towards Tafira Alta, take a right fork at the junction in the suburb itself, and continue for a short way along the minor road in the direction of Las Palmas; the entrance to the garden is just a few yards further on. Buses No 301 and 303 run every 15 minutes from the central bus station in Parque San Telmo, and stop near the main entrance; remember to tell the driver that you wish to get out here, however, as he will not stop unless you do so.

A WEALTH OF VEGETATION

Here you won't find the imported exotic flowers that adorn hotel gardens, but mostly species that grow only in these islands. Immediately past the main entrance are specimens of *Laurisilva* (bay laurel). Cool, damp forests of bay laurel used to cover much of the island before the Spanish conquest, but most of it is gone, destroyed by axes and chain saws. A few paces further on, the garden is planted with a completely different type of vegetation. Cacti and euphorbias, which thrive in the drier, low-lying regions of the island, extend their prickly branches high into the clear blue sky.

The garden, which was established in 1952 by the Swedish botanist Eric R. Sventenius, is laid out along the steeply sloping side of a gorge. The differences in height allow for a natural representation of the various climatic zones of Gran Canaria, and the typical plants and flowers for each type. Pines and cedars grow happily here beside margueritas, which occur in a number of variations on the island. Amid a riot of blossom, Jupiter's beard grows directly out of the rocks, and species of the endemic dragon tree, known as *drago,* have been planted in an avenue.

MINIATURE PARADISE

All sections of the garden can be reached by means of narrow paths, some of them fairly steep. They lead past waterfalls and cross a wooden bridge over a river. The variety of natural settings is as remarkable as the richness of the plant life on this small island, and the barrenness of the landscape today will arouse feelings of sadness that this miniature paradise has been destroyed.

Star Attraction
● **Jardín Canario**

Resist temptation
It is understandable that an amateur botanist might be tempted to try to cultivate some of these rare plants back home. In the interests of environmental protection, however, you should resist the temptation to take any part of any of the plants. It is strictly prohibited. Many garden centres offer seeds and seedlings which can be purchased and taken home. Even if you don't get to one of these outlets you can buy Canary Island seeds, or perhaps a little dragon tree, in one of the shops at the airport before you leave.

An overview of the garden

Map on pages 50–51

Below: harvest time, Agaete
Bottom: Teror

2: The North of the Island

Las Palmas – Teror – Agaete – Las Palmas (135km/84 miles)

The north is still the most important agricultural area of the island. The fertility of the soil stems from the clouds borne by the trade winds which bank up here in front of the central massif, bringing not only shade but also moisture. At altitudes over 800m (2,600ft), the average rainfall of 1,000mm (39 inches) per year means that this part of the island receives more rain than some areas of the British Isles. Nonetheless, its not sufficient to grow tropical fruits without irrigation, making agricultural alternatives few and far between. What is more, since Spain became a full member of the EU in 1995, it has been unable to offer an assured market for Canary Island bananas, which are a very small variety, and many of the banana plantations have been ploughed up. The result is that large tracts of land which were once fertile now lie fallow and are turning to scrub.

THE DONKEY'S BELLY

Gran Canaria's famous blue skies are more often obscured by clouds in the north of the island than in other regions. The area has acquired the nickname of '*la panza de la burra*' ('the donkey's belly') because it is said that in former times, a farmer would look for a shady place in which to have his midday siesta. If there was no tree available he would lie down beneath a donkey. When he looked up after his rest, he would see the grey shadow of the donkey's belly, bearing a strong resemblance to the trade-wind clouds.

TEROR

The first section of this route leads into the interior, leaving Las Palmas in a south-westerly direction along a short, newly-opened stretch of motorway, the GC-3, bypasssing Tamaraceite, a Guanche name meaning Grove of Palm Trees. Turn off onto the GC-21 (sometimes still marked as C817), which winds its way through a series of sharp bends to ★★★ **Teror**, a jewel of Canary Islands architecture, where distinguished town houses with elaborately carved window frames, doors and balconies have been well preserved.

MADONNA OF THE PINE TREE

Teror is Gran Canaria's principal religious centre and is the home of the Virgen del Pino, the island's patron saint. The miracle-working Madonna of the Pine Tree is said to have appeared to the local inhabitants on 8 September 1481 in a tree top. The little town has a number of lovely churches dedicated to the Virgin.

In the centre stands the 18th-century ★ **Basilica de Nuestra Señora del Pino** (open Mon–Fri 9am–noon, 2–6pm, Sat–Sun 9am–6pm), in which the Virgin is displayed in sumptuous clothing and jewellery, surrounded by votive gifts. She is still deeply revered, and pilgrims flock to Teror all the year round, but especially on her festival day, 8 September. A huge festival is held during the whole of that week, when lots of secular celebrations accompany the religious ceremonies and processions.

In front of the basilica stands the former Palacio Episcopal (Bishop's Palace), in which a cultural centre has been established.

> **Famous emigrants**
> The Plaza Teresa de Bolívar in Teror is named after the wife of the South American liberator, and founder of Bolivia, who originally emigrated to Venezuela from Teror. There she met Simón Bolívar, whose family had left war-torn Garachico in northern Tenerife to seek its fortune in South America, as did many Canary Islanders before and since.

Plaza Teresa de Bolívar, Teror

Map below

Finca de Osorio

The Finca de Osorio lies just outside Teror on the Arucas road. Here, an island government initiative supports a reforestation and conservation project in the extensive grounds of an old mansion, where courses and seminars are held. Laurel, which once covered the island, has been replanted, along with oak, chestnut, and other trees.

At weekends the estate and its attractive gardens can be visited, free (9am–5pm). Local people make a day of it and take a picnic. For visits at other times, tel: 928 630 090.

ARISTOCRATIC MUSEUM

To the right of the basilica, the ★ **Museo de Los Patrones de la Virgen del Pino** (open Mon–Thur and Sat 11.30am–7pm, Sun 10.30am–2pm; admission charge) is housed in a beautiful colonial building, set around a courtyard. Each room is furnished in the style of an aristocratic 17th-century home. It has belonged for most of that time to the Manrique de Lara family, who still come here for the festival week in September.

COBBLED ALLEYS AND MARKET STALLS

The centre of Teror is closed to traffic, which enables visitors to enjoy the traditional Canarian atmosphere in the cobbled alleys and little squares. A busy market is held in the town every Sunday morning, when goods for sale include not only fruit, vegetables and local cheeses, but also clothing and household articles. At other times there usually stalls behind the basilica selling both local produce and religious artefacts.

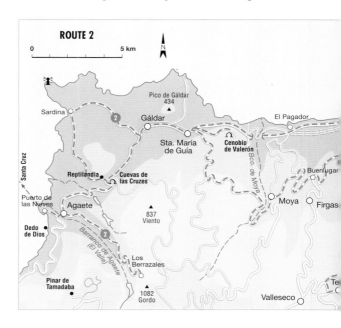

ARUCAS

Take the sinuous GC-43 north to ★ **Arucas**, the third-largest town on the island. It is dominated to the north by the **Montaña de Arucas** (402m/1,319ft), which has become a popular observation point.

There used to be an abundance of water around Arucas. At one time there was even a freshwater lake, so the area offered ideal conditions for the Spanish colonisers to cultivate sugar cane. A number of rum distilleries were also established, and the laurel trees that grew in profusion were felled to provide fuel. This first round of deforestation was one of the principal reasons for the water shortage on Gran Canaria.

ARUCAS RUM

Arucas is still famous for its rum production today, although the raw materials are now imported. The harvest from the tiny fields on which sugar cane is still grown is barely sufficient

Below: farmer, Arucas
Bottom: Arucas town

Map
on pages
50–51

*Below: Iglesia de
San Juan Bautista
Bottom: Arucas street scene*

to supply even local demand. Just outside the town the **Destileria Arehucas** welcomes visitors (open Mon–Fri 9.30am–1pm; free).

As with the whole of the northern part of the island, Arucas fell victim more than once to the problems of single-crop farming. The most recent example was the water-intensive banana plantations. Today, no more than 20 percent of the original area remains under cultivation; stiff competition from Central America has led to a sharp decline in demand.

SAN JUAN BAUTISTA

From the vast size of the church it is clear, however, how lucrative banana farming must have been for at least some of the local inhabitants. Built of black lava stone, the gigantic ★ **Iglesia de San Juan Bautista** was begun in 1909 and first used for worship in 1917. It was supposedly an imitation of Antoni Gaudí's unfinished Sagrada Família in Barcelona, and there are certainly some similarities, although the interior is more conservatively neo-Gothic. The most important work of art is the *Resting Christ* by the Canary Island sculptor, Manuel Ramos.

CASCO HISTORICO

Apart from visiting the church, it is also worth strolling through the attractive **Casco Histórico** (Historic Quarter), which was placed under a protection order in 1979, and through the manicured Parque Municipal with its exotic plants, at the top of the town. In a square by the park's entrance is a monument to the Canarian chief, Doramas, who is said to have met his end at the hands of the Spanish conqueror, Pedro de Vera, in 1491 on nearby Montaña de Arucas *(see page 37)*.

FIRGAS AND MOYA

Take the GC-300 (formerly C813/814) and after about 6km (4 miles) turn left in Buenlugar towards **Firgas**, a town of modest whitewashed

houses on the slopes of a hill, noted for its mineral water. The springs lie in the Las Madres Gorge (15km/9 miles south) and the product is widely available on all the Canary Islands.

At Buenlugar you could take the winding GC-350 to the little market town of **Moya**, which also has a church much larger and more impressive than the town seems to demand: **Nuestra Señora de Candelaria**.

A narrow road south, which should only be attempted in a four-wheel-drive vehicle, passes beautiful gorges and runs past the last 'wild' laurels in the island, which stretch along the valley floor. Access to the forest itself, called **Los Tilos de Moya**, is now forbidden, in an attempt to prevent further environmental damage. *Tilos* actually means lime trees, but there are none of these to be found here.

CENOBIO DE VALERON

The road from Moya wiggles across the Barranco de Moya towards the north coast and leads to the ★★ **Cenobio de Valerón** (open Wed–Sun 10am–5pm), one of the rare archaeological sites on the island that has any facilities for visitors. Some 300 caves, hollowed out of the volcanic rock, were for many years thought to have been a convent complex inhabited by *harimaguadas*, young women

Star Attraction
● Cenobio de Valerón

> **Island poet**
> Moya is known to islanders as the birthplace of their best-loved poet, Tomás Morales (1885–1921). His work was deeply influenced by the landscape and the sea. His house, close to the church, has been turned into a small but interesting museum (open Mon–Fri 9am–8pm, Sat–Sun 10am–2pm; free).

The steep approach to Cenobio de Valerón

Map on pages 50–51

being prepared for religious and wifely roles (*cenobio* means convent). However, it is now thought that the caves were granaries; their remote and elevated position made them easy to defend.

The caves are partly natural and partly man-made, hewn by the Guanches from the soft volcanic tufa. At one time they were closed by wooden doors and linked by passages and flights of steps. The complex is reached by a staircase, but can only be viewed from the outside because of the danger of rockfalls.

Back on the main road lies **Santa María de Guía**, a little town famous for its cheese, *queso de flor*. Try some in the cavernous store belonging to Santiago Gil Romero (Calle Marqués de Muni 34) whose family have been selling the product here for several generations.

Below: tufa caves,
Cenobio de Valerón
Bottom: Plaza de Santiago,
Gáldar

GALDAR

★ **Gáldar**, a few minutes' drive further on, is proud of its past. It is known as the Ciudad de los Guanartemes, or City of Rulers, because, before the Spanish conquest, it was the seat of one of Gran Canaria's two chiefs. His palace is believed to have occupied the site of the present church. The town was founded in 1484 and was the capital of Gran Canaria before Las Palmas. By the eastern entrance to the town, in the midst

of the confusion of traffic, stands a tall, narrow sculpture representing three Guanche princesses. There is another sculpture in the town depicting Tenesor Semidan, the last of the Guanche chiefs, who collaborated with the Spanish colonisers after being forcibly baptised. Almost all the names of the streets and squares hark back to the town's pre-Spanish past.

Gáldar has been slow to exploit the rich legacy of its past. Its pre-Hispanic sites, which archaeologists have been excavating for years, are still unfinished, but the town may soon become an interesting tourist destination.

THE CHURCH AND THE SQUARE

At first sight Gáldar does not seem a very inviting place. However, once you have reached the quiet square in front of the **Iglesia Santiago de los Caballeros**, with its shady trees, and a few chairs and tables around the kiosk, it is pleasant enough. The church was completed in 1872 but the font, now framed in wood, just to the right of the entrance, is thought to have been shipped over from Andalusia in the late 15th century. The church contains a number of statues attributed to sculptor José Luján Pérez (1756–1815) who was born in nearby Santa María de Guía.

Here, too, is the old **Ayuntamiento** (Town Hall). The spreading *drago*, or dragon tree, in its courtyard, claimed to be the oldest on the archipelago, rises above the roof of the building. It was planted in 1719, and there seems little room left for it to grow in any direction but upwards.

THE PAINTED CAVE

The 3-m (10-ft) high **Cueva Pintada** (Painted Cave), in the centre of town, is a relic from Guanche times that is considered a highly valuable discovery, as it is the only place on the islands where the cave walls have been decorated with coloured geometrical patterns. It is thought to have had a religious function. The cave is due to reopen in 2004 after many years

Guanche necropolis
Gáldar's other important archaeological site is the Poblado y Necrópolo de la Guancha, which was excavated in 1935, when numerous mummies were unearthed. It has been suggested that this was the burial place of Canarian Guanche nobles and royalty. It lies almost on the coast, reached via a narrow lane from the centre of town, running through banana plantations. However, it is only open to pre-booked groups (tel: 928 219 421 for details).

Iglesia Santiago de los Caballeros

Map on pages 50–51

Reptilandia
On the minor road leading south from Sardina, look out for signposts to Reptilandia (daily 11am–5pm). This is a reptile zoo in which snakes, crocodiles, tortoises and chameleons are kept in relatively natural surroundings.

Sardina

of renovation. An accurate replica of the cave can be seen in Las Palmas in the Museo Canario *(see page 33)*.

SARDINA

From the roundabout to the west of town, the main road to the right leads to **Sardina**, where a miniature resort has been established on a small beach protected by dark, volcanic rocks. Some of the houses in Sardina are actually cave dwellings. They are not obviously recognisable, as the present occupiers have constructed façades that make them look like ordinary houses. The harbour tavern, La Fragata, offers excellent fish dishes, where you can enjoy the beautiful view of the harbour from the dining room. The beach is popular with snorkellers.

Sardina is pretty quiet during the week but attracts people from Gáldar and Las Palmas at weekends, as well as some holiday-makers, mostly from mainland Spain. To the north of the village a lighthouse stands sentinel on the Punta de Sardina.

AGAETE

The main road south out of Gáldar, the C810, leads to the little town of ★ **Agaete** (if you made a detour to Reptilandia, carry on a short distance until you join the main road). The town guards the entrance to the most dramatic gorge on Gran Canaria, the Barranco de Agaete. Its narrow streets are lined with whitewashed houses with wooden balconies and, at the entrance to the town in the Plaza de la Constitución, stands the imposing **Iglesia de la Concepción**, colonial in style but actually 19th-century.

Near the church, off Calle Huertas, lies the **Huerto de las Flores** (open Mon–Fri 9am– 2pm), a small botanical garden containing some fine specimens of Canarian and tropical flowers. Its appeal also lies in its rare trees, which provide shade on a hot day. Narrow alleys lead away from the square in front of the church into the green, fertile gorge

THE BARRANCO DE AGAETE

Although the ★★**Barranco de Agaete** does not lie directly on the route, a detour into this enchanting valley should not be missed. The *barranco* (gorge) is signposted simply as *El Valle* (The Valley). Along the roadside lie several restaurants with terraces from which to enjoy the view. Visitors familiar with the neighbouring island of La Gomera will be reminded of the famous Valle Gran Rey. Here, too, you will find tiny terraced fields clinging to the steep sides of the valley, which has been transformed into a miniature tropical paradise.

Star Attraction
● **Barranco de Agaete**

Below: Barranco de Agaete
Bottom: Agaete

FRUIT AND MINERAL WATER

Whitewashed cottages are clad with luxuriant bougainvillaea in shades of lilac and red, and on the little plantations grow bananas, avocados, oranges, mandarins, mangoes and lemons, while lofty papaya trees border the river bed. Even coffee grows on the higher terraces. Towering in between are the lofty palm fronds of the Canary date palm. At the very top, on the cliffs, grows the Canary pine, with its needles up to 30cm (12in) long and its orange-yellow fruits.

There are some mineral springs in the upper section of the *barranco*; the water is bottled and sold. The spa amenities in the little village of **Los**

Map on pages 50–51

Berrazales were once popular, but have fallen into disrepair. There is a nice old hotel here, the Princess Guayarmina *(see page 123)*, which does offer spa treatments if they are booked in advance.

PUERTO DE LAS NIEVES

The landscape surrounding the little fishing village of ★★ **Puerto de las Nieves** is untamed and romantic, even dramatic in places. The Harbour of Snows lies just outside Agaete on the coast, which along this section drops several hundred metres steeply down to the sea. The village's name is less unusual than it appears, on an island where snow seldom falls. It refers to the chapel of the Virgen de las Nieves, the Madonna of the Snows, who is the patron saint of fishermen.

Below: locals at Puerto de las Nieves
Bottom: the dramatic coast

THE CHAPEL'S TREASURE

The chapel, known as the **Ermita de las Nieves**, looks like a doll's house compared with the massive sacred buildings elsewhere on the island. It houses a jewel of Flemish art: a 16th-century triptych attributed to Joos van Cleve, depicting the Virgin and Child flanked by saints Francis and Antony; ownership is shared with the church in Agaete. The wooden ceiling above the choir is adorned with remarkable *mudéjar* carvings.

The church is often closed but the key can be obtained from Señor Antonio, who lives at Calle Virgen de las Nieves 2; or ask in a neighbouring bar or shop where you can find him, or when the church is next likely to be open. However, Señor Antonio is very old and this arrangement may change in the near future.

Star Attraction
● **Puerto de las Nieves**

A PORT WITH A PAST

In the past, Puerto de las Nieves was a port of some consequence, when the agricultural produce of the whole Agaete area was shipped from here. Such bustling activity has largely ceased however, leaving just the red and blue fishing cutters to bob up and down beside the new jetty.

Below and bottom: beach and promenade, Puerto de las Nieves

There is, however, a regular ferry service run by the Fred Olsen line, that takes passengers to Santa Cruz de Tenerife (a free bus service from Parque Santa Catalina in Las Palmas connects with the port, *see page 115*).

A great deal of investment has gone into the harbour in recent years, in an attempt to attract visitors. The local economy is in a bad way as the fishing industry has declined, and tourism is seen as the way forward. The fishermen's wives may still sell the catch directly out of tin tubs by the roadside, as they have always done, but of the several hundred fishermen who once plied their trade here, only 50 remain, and even for them it is hard to make a living.

GRADUAL DEVELOPMENT

Puerto de las Nieves is gradually being developed, however, although some of the more radical plans have been blocked by environmentalists. A new promenade, the Paseo de los Poetas, has been built, and a number of low-rise apartment blocks and villas have sprung up behind it, blending quite nicely with the single-storey, whitewashed fishermen's cottages, with their brightly painted windows and doors. By the beach, docile camels and donkeys with saddles wait patiently for little riders, but on weekdays, the place is quiet.

Map on pages 50–51

There are a number of harbour-side taverns and restaurants that serve very good fish *(see page 110)*, and the village only really comes alive at weekends, when the residents of Las Palmas drive some 60 km (about 40 miles) to enjoy the atmosphere and the fresh fish. From Monday to Friday life moves at a comfortable pace, but what visitors see as a natural idyll represents economic ruin for those who live here.

Below: the Bajada de las Ramas ceremony
Bottom: Dedo de Dios

BRINGING DOWN THE BRANCHES

Puerto de las Nieves is famous for a festival celebrated with great enthusiasm by locals and visitors alike. This, like the triptych, is shared with the town of Agaete. Each year on 4–5 August, the residents of Puerto de las Nieves and Agaete gather fresh branches from the hillsides for the ceremony known as the **Bajada de las Ramas** ('Bringing Down the Branches').

Accompanied by music and traditional dances, they carry the branches to the harbour and whip the waves, then lay them at the feet of the Virgin of the Snows. Despite this nod towards the church, it is a ritual that has pagan origins and which is supposed to bring both rain and fertility. People come from all over the island to join in the fun, which goes on far into the night.

FINGER OF GOD

To the south of the village, the ★ **Dedo de Dios**, the Finger of God, is a prominent, bizarrely shaped pinnacle of rock rising from the sea. The formation is such a favourite motif for photographers that it has almost become a symbol of Gran Canaria. On the beach beneath it stands a popular restaurant that shares the same name.

BACK TO LAS PALMAS

The last leg of the journey, which has followed mostly winding roads, continues straight back along the coast road via Bañaderos to join the new stretch of motorway (GC-2) back to Las Palmas.

3: The East of the Island

Las Palmas – Caldera de Bandama – Telde – Las Palmas (90km/ 56 miles)

Map on page 62

Most visitors get to know this stretch of road immediately on arrival. Travelling along the east-coast motorway between Gando airport and Las Palmas to the north, or the tourist centres in the south, their gaze falls on barren piles of scree, dried-out river beds, industrial complexes and, in the distance, the plastic sheeting covering plantations of tomatoes, cucumbers or cut flowers.

Many are horrified: is this the holiday paradise of Gran Canaria? If, however, they look westwards towards the mountains, thejy will see how a dry, stony stream bed broadens out into a dramatic palm-fringed gorge. Many a village which at first sight looks uninviting may turn out to harbour remarkable cultural jewels. Well preserved cave dwellings tell of the ancient civilisation of the original Canary Islanders. So take a look behind the scenes and experience an authentic slice of Gran Canaria.

Below: cave dwellings in Barranco de Guayadeque
Bottom: view of Las Palmas from Pozo de Bandama

CALDERA DE BANDAMA

Leaving Las Palmas on the southwest arterial road in the direction of Santa Brígida, the GC-110 leads past Tafira Alta and you then take a left turn to the

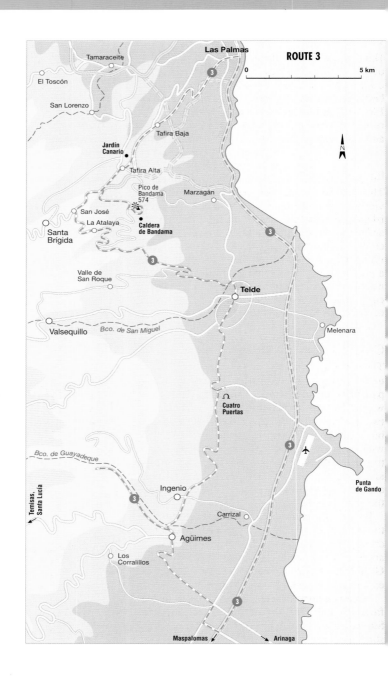

★★ **Caldera de Bandama**. The crater, which is 1km (½ mile) wide and 200m (655ft) deep, is one of the few places on the island where the volcanic origins of Gran Canaria can be seen clearly. The best view is from the volcanic peak next door, the **Pico de Bandama** (574m/ 1,883ft), which can be reached by car and has an observation platform and small bar.

ISLAND VIEWS

The observation platform provides magnificent views of the entire north and east coasts of the island, with the towns of Telde and Las Palmas, and the surrounding high-rise buildings, in marked contrast to the luxuriant gardens surrounding the villas of the exclusive Santa Brígida suburb. On a clear day it is sometimes possible to see the neighbouring island of Fuerteventura to the north-east, while the view to the west gives a foretaste of the scenic beauty of the central massif.

CLIMBING INTO THE CALDERA

The more adventurous can spend about 30 minutes climbing down into the crater itself via a steep path that is clearly visible from the rim. There you will find an old, abandoned farmhouse shaded by two enormous eucalyptus trees, and it is possible to make out the outline of a number of fields which are now lying fallow. Vines were once cultivated here. You can explore the base of the crater along the old tracks, where you might discover a spring and also a cave which was used to store the wine barrels.

South of the *caldera*, Spanish for cauldron and the international geological term for a volcanic crater, lies the largest golf course on the island, and the oldest one in Spain. The **Real Club de Golf de Gran Canaria** was founded by English expatriates at the end of the 19th century.

Visitors who wish to spend their holiday on the fairways will find the nearby **Hotel Escuela Santa Brígida** a suitable and pleasant place to stay *(see page 126)*.

Star Attraction
● **Caldera de Bandama**

Below: Caldera de Bandama
Bottom: Santa Brígida

Map on page 62

Agricultural centre
Telde has always been an agricultural centre, and the town council still holds a large cattle market during the second and third weeks of November. There are prizes not only for the biggest bull and the best-looking cow, but also for the nicest dog.

In the plaza at Telde

TELDE

Continuing south for a short distance along the road which now becomes the CG-15, turn left at San José along a pretty country road to ★ **Telde**. At first sight, the second-largest town on the island (pop. 82,000) looks like a modern, industrial development but the church of San Gregorio, which you see on entering the town, hints that there is more to Telde than meets the eye.

PROTECTED DISTRICTS

There are two distinct parts to Telde, the old and the new. The northern districts of San Juan and San Francisco have remained almost entirely free of modern development, and have been a protected conservation area since 1981. The plaza in front of the **Iglesia de San Juan Bautista** is particularly attractive. It is shaded by mature trees and surrounded by lovingly-restored, colonial-style houses with beautiful mosaic tiles and intricately carved balconies, built by merchants keen to demonstrate their wealth.

The local tourist office is situated in a little old house opposite the Plaza de San Juan. There is a small showroom devoted to local art and crafts (open Mon–Sat 9am–3pm). In a quiet street running off the square, brightly-coloured birds inhabit an aviary in a small play park.

PRECIOUS RELIC

The building of the church itself commenced in 1519, although the neo-Gothic towers were added at a much later date. The church houses a precious ★★**Flemish altarpiece** which has been integrated into a baroque altar. The six scenes from the life of the Virgin are regarded as the most valuable work of Canary Island art. The vast wealth resulting from the sugar-cane plantations, and later from the slave trade introduced by the Spanish colonisers, made possible the acquisition of this treasure in the 16th century.

Because the altarpiece is so valuable, the church is only open during services and for a while afterwards, when a guardian is on hand (daily from 5pm). The church also contains a very unusual image of Christ made from corn cobs and said to have been brought here from Mexico in the 16th century.

On a nearby street stands the **Casa del Conde de la Vega Grande**, which is now the town hall. Towards the end of the 1960s the count, whose family have greatly influenced the development of Gran Canaria across the centuries, began to transform his uneconomic estates in the south of the island into the largest tourist development project in the archipelago. The result is the biggest holiday complex in Europe, which has also earned the count a few millions *(see page 70)*.

FAMOUS BROTHERS

Another influential island family came from Telde. The brothers Juan and Fernando León y Castillo both contributed considerably to the economic development of the island during the 19th and early 20th centuries. Fernando became, among other things, foreign minister in the Spanish government, while Juan was an engineer who masterminded and directed the construction of the Puerto de la Luz, the port of Las Palmas. On each of the islands in the archipelago you will find at least one street named after the brothers.

Star Attraction
● **Flemish altarpiece**

Below: San Juan Bautista
Bottom: Telde mansion

Map on page 62

Their home town has dedicated a museum to them, the **Casa-Museo León y Castillo** (open Mon–Fri 9am–1pm; free), located in the street of the same name.

GUANCHE FOREBEARS

The history of Telde goes much further back than this. The belief that the legendary Guanche chief Doramas lived here may belong in the realm of myth, but there is no doubt that the region surrounding Telde was one of the principal settlements of the original islanders. Reports dating from the 16th century by the Italian military engineer Leonardo Torriani, who was commissioned by the king of Spain to fortify the islands against pirate attack, relate that there were 14,000 dwellings in huts and caves.

Below: Ingenio's church
Bottom: local goatherd

Two of the largest Guanche settlements reputedly lay in the Barranco de Telde: Tara in the north and Cendro in the south. Excavations in Tara unearthed the most important pre-Spanish sculpture on the island: the **Idolo de Tara**, the so-called 'First Mother'. Today it is on view in the Museo Canario in Las Palmas *(see page 32)*.

You can drive out to the site of the Guanche settlement, which lies on the western edge of town near the junction of the road to Valsequillo (on some maps shown as the Barranco de San

Miguel). It is hardly worth doing so, however, as the area has not been fenced off and is now used as an illegal rubbish dump and a home for goats.

INGENIO

Further along the GC-100 (although old milestones call it the C816), 8km (5 miles) from Telde, lies the attractive little town of **Ingenio**, which deserves a stopover. In Latin American Spanish, *ingenio* means sugar refinery, but it also means skill or ingenuity, and both meanings of the word are appropriate in this hardworking little town.

Here, during the 16th century, stood huge sugar presses, and it was sugar and the related distillation of rum that brought prosperity to the town. The industry declined long ago, and Ingenio now survives mostly on agriculture. In 1991, at the eastern entrance to the town, a monument of a sugar press was set up in memory of better times. A smartly tiled new plaza with modern fountains surrounds the attractive church of **La Candelaria**.

As you approach the town you will see the **Museo de Piedras y Artesania** (Museum of Stones and Handicrafts; open Mon–Fri 8am–6pm; free), which is mainly a showroom selling embroidered linen, pottery and ornaments.

> ### Hill of the Four Gates
> A Guanche site near Telde that can be recommended is the Montaña de las Cuatro Puertas (Hill of the Four Gates, 319m/1,047ft). It is easily accessible and lies near the GC-100 (C816), the road which leads southwards from Telde to Ingenio. Cuatro Puertas , which is believed to have been a Guanche cult site, consists of a main chamber with four entrances. Hollows and grooves in the stones indicate the existence of a place of sacrifice. The open space in front of the cave was a *tagoror*, a place of assembly. Some distance away, on the south side of the hill, are cave dwellings and storage places.

Ingenio's sugar roots

AGUIMES

Just 3 km (2 miles) further down the road is ★ **Agüimes**, which hides a jewel of an old town, immaculately restored (follow signs to the **Casco Histórico**). In the central Plaza de Nuestra Señora del Rosario there is a splendid church, the neo-classical San Sebastián, which houses sculpted figures of a number of saints by island sculptor, José Luján Pérez.

Agüimes stages a number of musical events in the summer and, as a convenient centre for walking, is a participant in the *turismo rural* scheme. Several traditional houses have been converted into small, comfortable hotels *(see page 123)*. The helpful little tourist office has an information centre with old photos and historical finds.

Map on page 62

> ### Cave dwellings
> Some of the cave dwellings in Gran Canaria have been occupied continuously since Guanche times. Others have been pressed into service in times of need – for example, after the Civil War (1936–39) when house building ground to a halt. These days, buying a 'second home' cave has become quite popular, and the property pages of the local papers sometimes carry advertisements for them.

Just to the west of Agüimes on the C815, in Los Corralillos, **Cocodrilo Park** (open Sun–Fri 10am–5pm) is home to a variety of crocodiles, snakes, scorpions and tropical fish, as well as zebras, leopards and llamas.

BARRANCO DE GUAYADEQUE

The ★★ **Barranco de Guayadeque**, whose steep mountain slopes are honeycombed with cave dwellings, is well worth a detour. Now under a protection order, it is one of the island's most beautiful valleys, where lush and rare Canarian flora still thrives. The best approach is from Agüimes, along the road signed to the **Centro de Interpretación** (open Tues–Sat 9am–5pm, Sun 10am–6pm; admission charge). The centre has some helpful background information on the valley and its people, and displays some of the items – pottery, bones and textiles – that have been recovered from caves in what was the most densely populated gorge on the island during Guanche times. More items are on display in the Museo Canario in Las Palmas *(see page 33)*.

Barranco de Guayadeque

CAVE VILLAGES

The cave villages are still occupied, although the population is diminishing. Now, as in days gone by, they constitute viable communities, of which the cave chapel is just as much a part as the cave bar or restaurant. These caves can be visited, and you will immediately notice the difference in climate on your skin. Travel agents in Las Palmas and in the southern resorts will organise excursions to the *barranco*, part of which is done on mule back. If you go alone, make sure you have the right clothes for the chilly heights, and plenty of water if you intend going far.

COMPLETING THE TRIP

The easiest route back to Las Palmas is to take the GC-100 from Agüimes towards Arinaga and rejoin the motorway heading north.

4: The South: a Mecca for Sun-Worshippers

San Agustín – Playa del Inglés – Maspalomas – Puerto de Mogán (70km/44 miles)

Here it is – Gran Canaria as it appears in the holiday brochures: miles of sandy beaches, bright blue skies, sand dunes and lagoons, crystal-clear Atlantic waters, high-rise hotels and bungalow complexes with luxuriant gardens around elegant swimming pools.

SOMETHING FOR EVERYONE

Apart from the guarantee of fine weather, there are plenty of reasons why tourism continues to boom in this part of the island: long beaches to walk along, clean water for bathing, stiff breezes for sailors and surfers, marinas for yacht owners and plenty of activities and diversions for children. Those in search of evening entertainment have a whole variety on offer, some of it lasting well into the early morning hours, and the adventurous have easy access to the wild gorges of the hinterland. You will find holiday flats in need of a coat of paint, five-star hotels with all the trimmings, and restaurants to suit every pocket: tapas bars and gourmet treats. The only thing you'll have difficulty in finding are lonely beaches.

Map on pages 70–71

Star Attraction
● **Barranco de Guayadeque**

Below: sea views
Bottom: Arguineguín

Map below

ARTIFICIAL CREATIONS

Until the 1960s there were no settlements at all along this stretch of the coast, apart from the poverty-stricken fishing villages of Puerto Rico, Arguineguín and Puerto de Mogán. Everything else has mushroomed out of the sand in the space of one generation, and everything was built just for tourists.

This artificial landscape was the initiative of a single man: the Conde del Castillo de la Vega Grande de Guadelupe, from Telde, who saw a way of turning his useless estates into a profitable gold mine. In 1962, the first complex was built in San Agustín, and in 1969 the development of El Oasis Maspalomas and Playa del Inglés began.

Before long the armies of building workers, by now financed by international tourist companies, had moved into every little bay and inlet. The projects were divided into various phases, all tastes were catered for and every kind of holiday dream can be discerned in the architecture along the coast. Puerto Rico attracts the sporty, San Agustín is for those in search of (relative) peace and quiet, and El Oasis is for the fashionable. Playa del Inglés is favoured by package tourists, while individual visitors prefer pretty Puerto de Mogán.

Beach restaurant

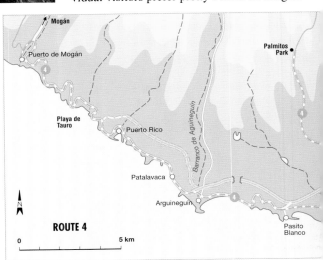

ROUTE 4

0   5 km

Mogán

Puerto de Mogán

Playa de Tauro

Puerto Rico

Patalavaca

Barranco de Arguineguín

Arguineguín

Palmitos Park

Pasito Blanco

N

REACHING THE COAST

Leave Las Palmas on the motorway GC1 going south, and after 40km (25 miles) you will think you have entered another big city. (If you are coming direct from the airport, it is only about 24 km/15 miles.) Multi-lane highways and high-rise buildings appear, with only the odd patch of artificial green in between, and seldom an unobstructed view of the beach and the sea – the so-called Costa Canaria is one vast *urbanización*.

SAN AGUSTÍN

The best seaside resorts and most attractive beaches are strung along the coast like a necklace. The first of any real interest is ★ **San Agustín**, lying at the heart of the southern tourist region. This, the first of the resorts, was planned from the start to appeal to the discriminating visitor, and this is still obvious, although San Agustín is showing its age now.

The 50-odd apartment complexes have spacious, well-kept gardens, some with swimming pools. The coast road divides the development into two sections – the lower one by the beach and the upper one on the hillside. The latter has excel-

Nueva Europa
Close to the little resort of Playa del Águila, you will see signs to the holiday village of Nueva Europa, which is not quite as new as the name would have you believe. A relatively small complex of holiday homes with a private, sheltered beach, it was built for visitors who prefer a quiet holiday. It has its restaurants and supermarkets, though for nightlife you'll have to drive to Playa del Inglés, 5km (3 miles) away.

Nueva Europa is best known for the popular wind-surfing school belonging to the Danish Dunkerbeck family. The regular northeast trade winds make conditions in the bay ideal.

Burial games

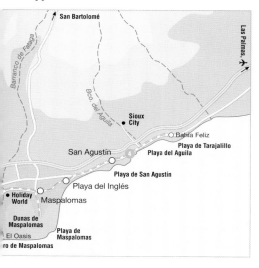

Culture in the sun
Although Playa del Inglés and Maspalomas are undeniably tourist creations, the efficient local municipal authority, based in San Bartolomé de Tirajana, does all it can to ensure that they are not cultural deserts. There is a regional folk festival in late May, a wide programme of events called Maspalomas in Summer that includes children's activities, a 'summer university' and jazz concerts; and a well-regarded film festival at the end of October.

Playa del Inglés

lent views across the bay, and from some places you can even see as far as the white dunes of Maspalomas, although there is a main road to cross (via a foot bridge) and a longer walk to the sea.

The beach is sheltered and ideal for children. San Agustín has some sports facilities: sailing, golf and riding, and a few beach-side bars and restaurants, but it remains relatively quiet. A continuation of San Agustín as you head towards Playa del Inglés is **Playa de las Burras**, known locally as **Playa Chica**, the Little Beach.

PLAYA DEL INGLÉS

★★ **Playa del Inglés**, the largest tourist centre on the south coast, has some 350 bars and restaurants, 250 holiday apartment complexes, 50 discos and 20 large hotels. The main attraction, of course, is the long, white-sand beach, lined with bright umbrellas, which extends for over 8km (5 miles), with sand dunes reaching to the Maspalomas lighthouse.

The scorching-hot beach is so large that even in summer there is plenty of room for the thousands of visitors. The only really crowded area is likely to be the water's edge, which can become a bit of a crush. Overhead, bi-planes trail streamers advertising clubs and discos, while out at sea wind-surfers and water-skiers put on a free show.

Paralleling the beach – which is reached via steps or escalators from the attractive cliff-top promenade – is a long commercial strip lined with fast-food outlets, smart restaurants, German pubs and tea rooms, video arcades and shops full of sunhats, sarongs and beach balls.

SHOPPING CENTRES

When it was built in the 1960s, the high-rise developments made Playa del Inglés the last word in modernity. It looks like a dormitory suburb, with broad streets, mostly multi-storey buildings, and three vast shopping centres as well as a number of smaller ones. The oldest of the three, the Kasbah (Avenida de España), has retained a certain individual charm. The two others, Yumbo and Citá, could be on the outskirts of almost any new town development anywhere in Europe.

As well as a huge variety of shops, they have plenty to attract the post-beach crowd during the evening, with restaurants, bars, amusement arcades and discos galore. On the edge of town it is much quieter and buildings are lower. Close to the dunes, in the direction of Maspalomas, lie mainly residential areas with large villas.

Star Attraction
● **Playa del Inglés**

MASPALOMAS

★ **Maspalomas** lies at the western end of Playa del Inglés. Inland, the two resorts merge almost imperceptibly, while their seaside areas are divided by the golf course and the great stretch of dunes. Maspalomas is some 10 years younger than its neighbour, and has a predominance of bungalow complexes and single-storey holiday flats set in gardens with swimming pools. In order to set themselves apart from the earlier developments, the builders of Maspalomas chose a rustic style with plenty of landscaped open spaces and an 18-hole golf course.

Below and bottom: aspects of Maspalomas

The disadvantage of this more space-conscious resort lies in the greater distances between the facilities. As the street names indicate, much of Maspalomas was built by tour operators so you

Map on pages 70–71

Playa de Maspalomas

> **The Charco**
>
> El Charco, the Maspalomas lagoon that is part of the nature reserve, is surrounded by a belt of vegetation which used to be a refuge for numerous migratory birds en route to Africa. Frightened away by so much human activity, many stopped coming, but are now being encouraged back. There are few nesting species left, but the moorhen has returned and it is hoped that others will follow.
>
> Close to the lagoon is the remnant of a once-lush palm grove. Efforts are being made to preserve the remaining Canarian palms and to reintroduce other species.

may find yourself in Avenida Touroperador Neckermann or Kuoni, or even Avenida Saga Tours.

THE DUNES

Although the ★★ **Dunes of Maspalomas** are the main attraction along the Costa Canaria, they are often disrespectfully described by local people as 'the desert'. In fact, the mountains of sand are a spectacular sight. Some of them are tens of metres high and cover an area of 4sq km (1½sq miles). At the far end stands a lighthouse *(faro)* which is 56m (184ft) high and more than 100 years old. The sand dunes were designated a nature reserve in 1994, to preserve and restore their ecosystem, so visitors are asked to keep to the marked paths.

It is often claimed that the bright yellow sand was blown across to Gran Canaria from the Sahara. In fact, it originally came from the sea. At one time Gran Canaria was 90m (96yds) wider at this point. The coast was torn away by the sea and then re-deposited along with the dunes. The sand was formed to a large extent from the shells of crustaceans which have been ground to a fine powder by wind and waves.

EL OASIS

To reach the beach and dune area, take the long Avenida Oceania that runs alongside the Barranco de Maspalomas. This brings you to the lighthouse and to the smart end of the resort, ★ **El Oasis**, where the palm-lined Paseo Marítimo runs beside the sea and borders a shallow lagoon, the Charco de Maspalomas, which is fed by seawater as well as freshwater from the nearby gorge. The area provides a haven and breeding place for many bird species *(see box)*.

Here, the elegant hotels and bungalows tucked away between garden-fringed streets are still regarded as the jewel of Gran Canaria's entire tourist area. Among the most splendid and luxurious are the Hotel Maspalomas Oasis, the Gran Hotel Costa Meloneras and the Grand Hotel Residencia *(see pages 124–5)*.

EXCURSIONS AND ENTERTAINMENTS

After so much sand and sun, you may long for a little variety. Excursions can easily be made to a number of amusement parks and other attractions in the vicinity. A big favourite, with both adults and children, to the northeast of San Agustín is ★ **Sioux City** (open Tues–Sun 10am–5pm; barbecues Fri 8am; admission charge), which can be reached by following a side road leading up into the mountains from the motorway near Playa del Águila. Bus No 29 runs from Maspalomas and Playa del Inglés.

Star Attraction
● **Dunes of Maspalomas**

Below and bottom: the sand dunes of Maspalomas

WESTERN ATMOSPHERE

The very name, Sioux City, conjures up Buffalo Bill, and the landscape – the Cañon del Águila (Eagles' Gorge) with its arid, steppe-like vegetation – forms an ideal backdrop for the Western town, complete with saloon, bank and numerous other buildings which look so authentic that you expect John Wayne to appear any minute.

A number of films have been shot in the streets and in front of the corral. Bank raids and cattle drives are staged regularly throughout the day, and on Friday evening there is a barbecue night with live country music. This theme park has been operating since 1972 and the right mix of entertainment has been perfected over the years.

Map
on pages
70–71

Below: baking on the beach
Bottom: cooling off
at Aqua Sur

WORLDS OF FUN

Holiday World (open daily from 6pm till late; admission charge) is a vast amusement complex in the Campo Internacional, on the way into Maspalomas. It offers every imaginable distraction: a laserdrome, numerous rides including a giant wheel and a big dipper; a sea lion show, open-air dance floor and lots of bars and fast-food outlets. Also in the Campo Internacional is **Ocean Park** (open daily 10am–5.30pm; admission charge) with all the usual aquatic amusements: artificial waves, water slides and a lake, plus video games, a hamburger bar and other places to eat.

PALMITOS PARK AND AQUA SUR

★★**Palmitos Park** (open daily 10am–6pm; admission charge) is an artificial oasis filled with sub-tropical plants and covering an area of 200,000sq m (239,000sq yds). It lies some 10km (6 miles) north of Maspalomas and is signposted from the motorway. There are frequent buses from Playa del Inglés and San Agustín (No 45) and Maspalomas Faro and Puerto Rico (No 70).

Between steep slopes dotted with euphorbia, ponds were dug and 45 species of palm tree planted, along with agaves and cacti. The park has become the home of 1,500 species of exotic birds. Particularly popular attractions include demon-

strations of birds of prey in flight, the butterfly house, the orchid house, the aquarium, containing 300 species of exotic fish, and the parrot shows, held several times a day, in which the birds perform a variety of tricks.

On the road up to Palmitos Park, about 3 km (2 miles) from Maspalomas, is the largest water park on the island, **Aqua Sur** (open daily in summer 10am–6pm, until 5pm in winter; admission charge; buses as for Palmitos Park). It has numerous water rides and slides, a wave pool, several large swimming pools and children's pools as well as all the usual shops and fast-food stalls. Guaranteed to keep children happy for hours.

PASITO BLANCO

Leaving the major resorts and heading west, you will come to **Pasito Blanco**, which lies south of the road beside the sea. It owes its significance as a marina to its pretty little bay, which has been developed as a leisure boating centre and yacht club (tel: 928 142 194).

ARGUINEGUIN

Next come Arguineguín and Patalavaca, which mark the start of the administrative district of Mogán. Here the landscape changes. The coast no longer consists of long, white beaches but becomes steep and rocky with numerous small bays with darker sand. The airborne sand, which can make sunbathing on the eastern beaches unpleasant during periods of 'Africa weather', does not penetrate into these sheltered coves.

Arguineguín is recognisable from afar because of its cement factory, and does not receive many holidaymakers. Cruise ships use it as a port of call, but their passengers are whisked off in coaches to the nearby resorts. However, it is a pleasant enough little town, albeit not very exciting, and its whitewashed houses are bright with flowers. It is still a working fishing port and retains the individuality of a long-established community, which can be a relief after the big-resort bustle.

Star Attraction
● Palmitos Park

Space Centre
To the west of Maspalomas you will notice the bulky domes and huge antennas of the NASA space centre (not open to the public). It was from here that the first moon landing by the US astronaut Neil Armstrong was tracked and other Mercury and Apollo missions observed.

Arguineguín

Map
on pages
70–71

The neighbouring enclave of **Patalavaca** is immediately recognisable by the hotel complexes, built by luxury chains, that sprout out of the hillside along the rocky coast. Since they are not high-rises, the sea views are unimpaired. The developers have not attempted to economise, and the cleverly planned schemes more than compensate for the somewhat unattractive location.

PUERTO RICO

★★ **Puerto Rico** is the small, sport-loving alternative to Playa del Inglés, which by now is some 20km (13 miles) behind you. There are no high-rises to spoil the view, but the apartment blocks rise in serried ranks up the steep slopes of a gorge which opens onto a semi-circular, sandy bay.

Below and bottom:
Puerto Rico developments

The harbour is Spain's sailing mecca. Members of the local sailing school have managed to bring home five Olympic gold medals (three from Barcelona and two from Los Angeles). The town council has expressed its thanks by naming streets after the winners.

The most important sport of all here, however, and one in which even beginners can indulge, is deep-sea fishing. Fast boats take groups of four to six anglers out to the well-stocked waters, where dolphins and tuna and – less frequently than would-be heroes would have one believe – even sharks can be seen *(see page 113)*.

There is bottom-fishing available all year round, but the deep-sea season is summer, when tuna and marlin can be caught. This sport, too, has brought Puerto Rico its share of fame and honour: local fishermen can lay claim to 34 world records in deep-sea fishing.

Diving is also popular, with facilities for beginners as well as the experienced *(see page 113)*.

FAMILY RESORT

This is very much a family resort, and a slightly more up-market one. There's not a lot happening in the town centre, apart from a small park that is a riot of exotic flowers, and a vast shopping complex in which the tourist information office is also to be found. Swimming is not exciting here, as the bay is protected by moles and the beach created by bringing in lorry-loads of sand, but it is safe for children. Puerto Rico's other attraction is the popular **Aquapark**, which has what it said to be the longest water slide in the world.

PLAYA DE TAURITO

Playa de Taurito, a little further west, is elegant in blue and white with marble everywhere. Individual visitors as well as those on all-inclusive holidays are welcome. The elaborately designed swimming complexes with various pools, waterfalls and suspension bridges, built by the community for the benefit of hoteliers and their well-to-do customers, are open to the public.

PUERTO DE MOGAN

★★★ **Puerto de Mogán**, at the far end of Gran Canaria's southern coastal road, is the jewel of Gran Canaria's tourist-development policy. Not so long ago, old men gathered to reminisce by the quayside, and strangers were hardly seen. Today, the main road winding through the village has become busy with tourists. Until as recently as the early 1980s, rusty boats bobbed on the waves

Star Attractions
● **Puerto Rico**
● **Puerto de Mogán**

Boat trips
There is plenty of seaborne activity, even for those who don't sail or fish themselves. Boats run by Lineas Salmón (tel: 649 919 383) and Blue Bird (tel: 928 224 151) make pleasant voyages between Arguineguín, Puerto Rico and Puerto de Mogán.

Stylish detailing at Puerto de Mogán

Map
on pages
70–71

Friday market

On Friday morning a huge market is held around the old port in Puerto de Mogán. Here you can buy African carvings, brightly-coloured sarongs and mirrored sunglasses, as well as a variety of local produce and exotic soaps and oils, and be entertained by musicians and jugglers. Get here early if you don't like crowds: by 10.30am coaches will have deposited hundreds of tourists from the nearby resorts.

Boats in the harbour

in the harbour. Once an unassuming little place with a population of only 400, Puerto de Mogán has been transformed into the island's most successful tourist project, but development has been kept within reasonable bounds.

LITTLE VENICE

Puerto de Mogán is advertised as 'Little Venice'. There are arched bridges spanning the little canals and alleys. Bordering the quayside are whitewashed, two-storey houses in typical local style with brightly coloured paintwork and wrought-iron balconies. Vibrant bougainvillaea grows in profusion, hibiscus nods over garden walls and window boxes are bright with geraniums.

There is an old fishing port and a new leisure port, the ★★ **Puerto Deportivo**, with moorings for more than 200 yachts, some very smart indeed. The colonial-style port authority building overlooks the latter.

The narrow streets and pretty squares are all pedestrianised, and numerous cafés, bars and restaurants tempt visitors to linger. Most have menus in English and German, and several offer English afternoon tea, or German apple cake.

Thousands of day trippers from other parts of the island come to wander through the romantic alleys, admire the fountains and old-fashioned street lamps, and pose for photographs in front of the luxury yachts.

THE BAY AND THE BEACH

There is a diving school here, for the more adventurous; or visitors can take a trip around the bay (boats leave from near the port authority building); or embark on a journey through the underwater world in a bright yellow, glass-bottomed submarine (tel: 928 565 108), which allows a good view of fish and aquatic plants.

The local dark-sand beach, Playa de Mogán, is being extended and covered in layers of fine, lightly-coloured sand, and a breakwater ensures that it's a safe bathing area for children.

5: The West: Unspoilt Nature

Puerto de Mogán – Veneguera – San Nicolás de Tolentino – Agaete (90km/56 miles)

Apart from the broad Barranco de San Nicolás de Tolentino and the little village of Veneguera on the coast, the western region of Gran Canaria is virtually uninhabited, and thus appropriately described as the 'Wild West'. Except for a single tongue of land, the beach at Veneguera, the magnificent scenery which ends in the craggy inlets of the steep west coast, has all been declared a conservation area.

SPLENDID SLOPES

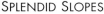

To the west and south, as far as the eye can see, extends an endless succession of gold, grey and red cliffs. On the slopes of Los Azulejos, the green discolouration reveals where the iron in the rocks has been oxidised. On the upper slopes grows the Canary pine, but on the drier, lower reaches, the only vegetation consists of the *tabaibas*, which have adapted to the arid climate, euphorbias and prickly pears, which traditionally provided the food of the cochineal beetle. The few isolated farmhouses are almost all derelict, and many of the walls supporting the terraced fields have fallen into disrepair.

Map on page **82**

Star Attraction
● **Puerto Deportivo**

Below: colourful countryside
Bottom: the road through the Barranco de Mogán

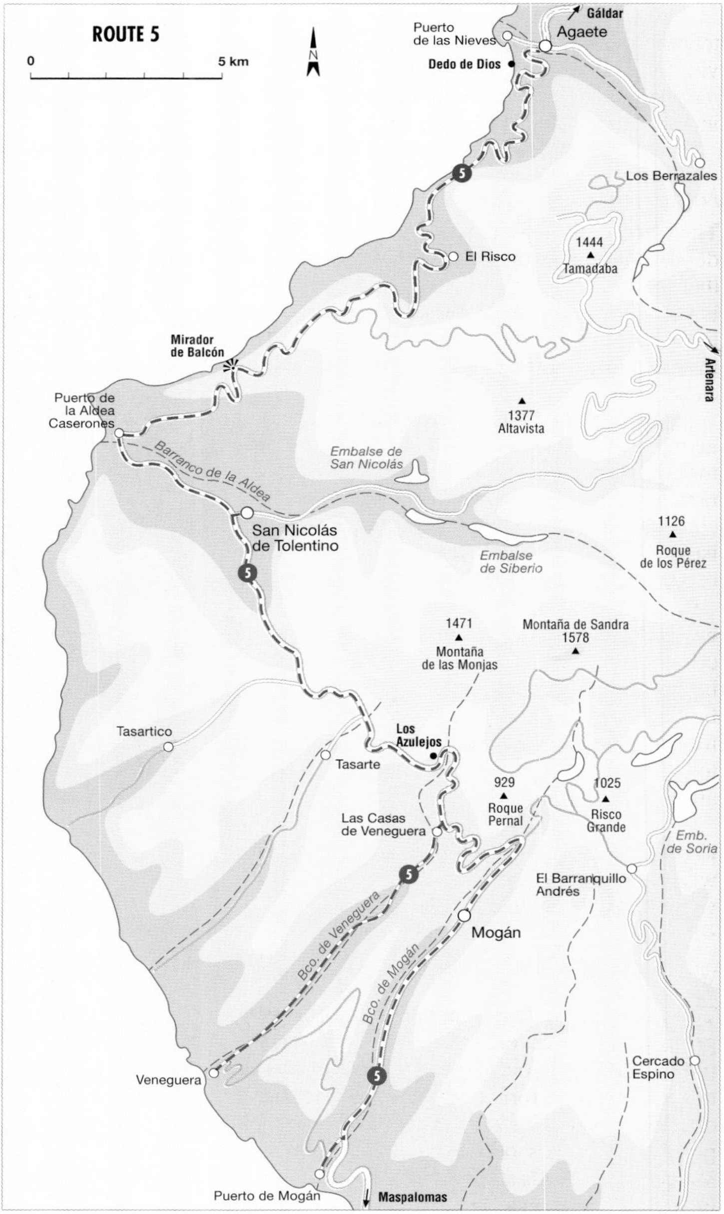

ROUTE 5

0   5 km

N

→ Gáldar
Agaete
Puerto
de las Nieves
Dedo de Dios •

Los Bernazales

5

○ El Risco

▲ 1444
Tamadaba

→ Artenara

**Mirador
de Balcón**

Puerto de
la Aldea
Caserones

Barranco de la Aldea

▲ 1377
Altavista

*Embalse de
San Nicolás*

San Nicolás
de Tolentino

5

*Embalse
de Siberio*

1126
▲
Roque
de los Pérez

1471
▲
Montaña
de las Monjas

Montaña de Sandra
1578
▲

Tasartico ○

**Los
Azulejos** ●

Tasarte ○

929
▲
Roque
Pernal

1025
▲
Risco
Grande

*Emb.
de Soria*

Las Casas
de Veneguera ○

El Barranquillo
Andrés

5

Bco. de Veneguera

Bco. de Mogán

Mogán

Veneguera ○

5

Cercado ○
Espino

Puerto de Mogán ○

↓ **Maspalomas**

If you have always wanted to hire a jeep, this tour of the lonely mountains of Gran Canaria provides an ideal opportunity. However, even an ordinary small car should be able to cope with the inclines, albeit at a more sedate pace.

Map opposite

MOGAN

The first section of road, which leads from Puerto de Mogán through the **Barranco de Mogán** into the interior, is still easy territory, although the road is a winding one. The products of this fertile valley are often offered for sale along the roadside: in season you may see passion fruit, papaya, avocados, mangoes and guavas.

Barranco de Mogán

Until the early 1970s, the town of **Mogán**, situated at the upper end of the valley (about 12 km/8 miles from the coast), was nothing more than a remote mountain village. Despite the fact that the community of Mogán covered the largest administrative district on the island, it could only be reached by winding footpaths.

Today, a number of artists, craftspeople and writers have settled here, and, as it has been discovered by foreign visitors as well, the place has become quite prosperous. Owing to the plentiful supply of water in the valley, the gardens are luxuriant, and a few residents advertise rooms to let. Some of the restaurants in the village are also worth stopping for.

Beyond Mogán a track leads to several inland lakes. This mountain landscape is a paradise for walkers, although the noise of four-wheel drive vehicles does tend to shatter the idyll.

VENEGUERA

The C810, which from this point becomes progressively more adventurous (despite what some maps would have you believe), turns first towards the southwest, before continuing in a northerly direction again. After some 5km (3 miles), a signposted road leads off down the Barranco de Veneguera and ends at the little Moorish-type village of ★ **Veneguera**. From there a rough track

Below: negotiating barrancos
Bottom: fishing at Veneguera

(only suitable for four-wheel drives and very determined drivers) leads down to the sea, almost petering out towards the end. Visitors in search of empty beaches on Gran Canaria can find what they are looking for here and in the neighbouring bays. Veneguera is still lonely and tranquil, its fine dark sand inviting bathers. The neighbouring, and even more inaccessible, beaches at the end of the **Barrancos de Tasarte** and **Tasartico**, by contrast, are steep and stony.

ENVIRONMENTAL CONCERNS

For some years Veneguera was the subject of a major battle over plans to build an up-market holiday complex. Environmental lobbyists belonging to ASCAN (Spain's largest environmental and nature protection agency) and various other groups succeeded in delaying the scheme, and in 2003 Veneguera was saved when it was incorporated in the Roque Nublo Rural Park.

DESERTED AREA

Visitors with four-wheel drive vehicles may like to try the descent to some of the other *barrancos* leading down to this stretch of coast. Each of them a miniature paradise, the gorges are contained by steep rock faces, and the valley floors are covered with clumps of waist-high reeds and palm trees. There are also little plantations of bananas, papayas and citrus fruits. After skidding along the gravel for some way you will eventually reach the sea and the tranquillity of the island's last empty beaches.

The countryside was rather less idyllic for those who were once forced to make a living from the harvest provided by the narrow strip of land along the gorge floors. There are numerous abandoned farmhouses and terraces lying fallow. In 1950, the Barranco de Veneguera housed 700 registered inhabitants. Fewer than 100 are left today, and these are almost all older people; their children and grandchildren have moved out to find work elsewhere.

SAN NICOLAS DE TOLENTINO

Returning to the C810, which winds its way through countless sharp bends past coloured rock walls, including the bright green rocks at the Fuente de los Azulejos (tracks to the beaches of Tasarte and Tasartico lead off to the left), the route continues to **San Nicolás de Tolentino**. Since 1991, this agricultural centre has been known officially as La Aldea de San Nicolás, but the local population is not keen to accept the new name.

Above the town the steep mountain walls recede to make way for a broad valley. The main crops grown here are tomatoes and cucumbers, as adequate water supplies are available from the huge storage reservoirs to the east of the village. Until a few years ago, the aromatic Canary Islands tomatoes held their own against their Dutch competitors. Recently, however, the market has also been contested by Morocco, which can supply the EU with early tomatoes at lower prices.

STRUGGLING TO SURVIVE

San Nicolás also suffers from the migration of its inhabitants. Since the mid-1980s, more than 20 percent of the almost 7,000 residents of this fertile valley have left their homes. The ambitious local tourist-development plans have not been

> **Cactualdea**
> Shortly before reaching San Nicolás, at Tocodomán, you will see signs to Cactualdea (Cactus Village; open daily 10am–6pm; admission charge). Here there is an extensive range of well-labelled cacti, planted among palms and *drago* trees. As an added draw, there are camel rides, occasional displays of *lucha canaria*, a replica Guanche cave and a 'mineral mine' with stones for sale. There are also wine tasting sessions and a restaurant that specialises in typical Canarian cooking.

San Nicolás de Tolentino

Map
on page
82

realised, and younger people see little future in this remote community.

The town is trying its best, however. There is a small **Museo Vivo** (Living Museum; appointment required, tel: 928 892 485) just before you enter the town, where rural ways of life are demonstrated. The little tourist office has cheerful leaflets on local crafts – traditional pottery and woven textiles with strong Latin American influences – but the opportunities they mention, to watch local craftspeople at work, no longer apply.

Playa de la Aldea

PUERTO DE LA ALDEA

The **Puerto de la Aldea** (Port of the Village) has a steep, rocky beach and a small, sandy cove. There are several modest but well-regarded fish restaurants, a tiled promenade that has been some years in the making, a shady little park with picnic tables and a children's playground.

At the end of the park and promenade lies a little lagoon, the *charco*, which looks completely unprepossessing, but on 11 September each year it is the site of the ancient **Fiesta del Charco**, a rowdy event in which people attempt to catch fish with their hands and end up throwing each other into the water. Bouts of stick fighting and *lucha canaria* (wrestling) are also part of this odd but good-natured festival.

When no such celebrations are taking place, this is a nice spot to watch the sun set behind Mount Teide on neighbouring Tenerife.

INTO THE HILLS

There is a detour to the interior that can only be recommended to visitors with four-wheel-drive vehicles and experience of travelling across remote mountain tracks. If you turn off into the Barranco de la Aldea near San Nicolás, following the single-track road up the gorge and passing a number of *embalsas* (reservoirs) on the way, you will eventually join Route 6 to the west of Artenara *(see page 89)*. The trip is an arduous but rewarding one.

MIRADOR DE BALCON

The rocky coastline stretching away to the north
of Puerto de la Aldea is splendid. The cliffs plunge
several hundred metres almost vertically down to
the sea, scaled only by a hair-raising, serpentine
road. The road has been widened on a couple of
the hairpin bends to create observation points. The
first, the ★★ **Mirador de Balcón**, is particularly
impressive and should be included in any tour
of the western part of the island.

On a clear day you can make out the snow-
capped tip of Mount Teide on Tenerife (3,718m/
12,200ft), the highest mountain not only in the
Canary Islands but in the whole of Spain. A short
way further along, the **Andén Verde**, which is
being widened, also offers fantastic views.

THE WAY BACK TO BASE

The coast road continues to curl around the cliffs
until it finally drops down into Agaete *(see page
56)*. If you are heading back to Las Palmas, you
should follow the main road from Agaete, which
links up with the GC-2 motorway for the stretch
past Gáldar and along the coast. If you are based
in one of the southern resorts then you must
retrace your route. The advantage is that you will
now be a little more familiar with the road and
better able to appreciate the stunning views.

Star Attraction
• **Mirador de Balcón**

*Below: fishing boat,
Playa de la Aldea
Bottom: Mirador de Balcón*

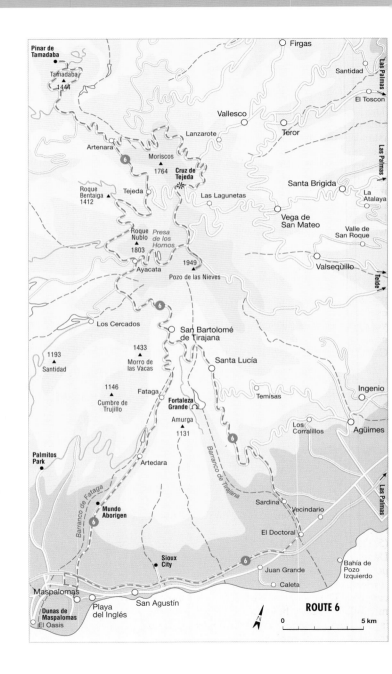

6: The Centre: Tempest of Stone

Playa del Inglés – Roque Nublo – Artenara – Santa Lucía and back (200km/125 miles)

The Spanish writer and philosopher Miguel de Unamuno (1864–1936) called the centre of the island 'the tempest of stone'. The rocks shimmer in shades of red, yellow, gold and blue: precipices, monoliths rising heavenwards like giant fingers, jagged peaks, cliffs and cones. Over millions of years volcanic eruptions, wind and rain have moulded the country into every bizarre form imaginable. It is a wild, majestic setting which impresses everyone who sees it.

Map opposite

Below: Cruz de Tejeda
Bottom: Roque Nublo

ROCKS AND VILLAGES

The formation of the island took place over a long period of time. The oldest rock samples have been estimated at 16 million years old, while the youngest are only 3,000 years. In contrast to its neighbour, La Palma, the volcanoes of Gran Canaria are considered to be extinct.

In this landscape gleaming white villages cling to the rock, like Tejeda, or are carved out of it, like Artenara. From the roof of the island the view extends out across the sea to Tenerife, where Mount Teide, snow-capped in winter, hovers in the mist.

THE HIGHEST PEAKS

The highest peaks on the island lie in the centre. The Pico de las Nieves (Peak of Snows) is the highest of all at 1,949m (6,394ft), followed by the Roque Nublo, the Rock of Clouds, at 1,803m (5,915ft), and Roque Bentaiga (1,412m/4,632ft). Deep *barrancos* radiate out from this central point, descending to sea level at the coast.

Five main gorges branch out into 26 smaller canyons. These gorges, created by erosion over millions of years, have always served as the island's main arteries. Their fertile soil nurtures tropical and sub-tropical fruits, on their slopes

Map on page 88

grow the elegant pine trees, and at the very top perch the undemanding almond trees whose blossoms clothe the rugged landscape in a cloud of pink in January and February. As well as almonds, figs and citrus fruits are harvested, and potatoes and other vegetables grown. Cattle are also kept, and it is quite possible that your way may suddenly be blocked by a herd of sheep or goats.

PROTECTING THE LANDSCAPE

Below: locals of Artenara
Bottom: camel safari, Fataga

Before the Spanish conquered the island some 600 years ago, mountain peaks rose above dense pine forests. Centuries of indiscriminate felling have destroyed not only the trees, but also the streams and rivers which once made Gran Canaria so fertile. Near Santa Lucía or Fataga you get a glimpse of how green and lovely the island once was.

At least the *pinar*, the pine forest, has been brought back to life by a reforestation project near Tamadaba. Lichens, which hang from the trees like beards, show that the forest's worst enemy of our industrial times, air pollution, has not yet penetrated as far as this. The pine trees have a good chance of survival.

Much of central Gran Canaria is now a protected area, a *parque natural*. While farmers are still allowed to cultivate their fields here, they are not allowed to enlarge them.

BARRANCO DE FATAGA

Visitors crossing the island from the south should leave the motorway near Playa del Inglés, in the direction of Fataga (starting from Las Palmas, the route can be followed in the opposite direction). After a short while, golden-coloured walls of rock with broad, pillar-like bands of basalt seem to crowd in on the **Barranco de Fataga**, somewhat reminiscent of the canyons featured in Hollywood Westerns. As the altitude increases, the valley becomes greener. Plantations of tropical fruits are spread out across the valley floor, and palm trees with feathery crowns grow along the roadside.

About 5km (3 miles) up is ★ **Mundo Aborigen** (open daily 9am–6pm; admission charge), an open-air museum that recreates the lifestyle and customs of the Guanches. It's a bit of a theme park, but very well done, and manages to be both educational and entertaining. Bus No 18 runs from San Fernando (just outside Playa del Inglés) several times a day.

A little further up the road is the **Camel Safari Park** (open daily 9am–6pm; admission charge), where visitors can take camel rides

FATAGA AND SAN BARTOLOMÉ

About 8km (5 miles) from Mundo Aborigen, you reach ★ **Fataga**, built on a precipitous rock jutting out into the gorge. The little village has no historical sights, but there's a nice church and the pretty streets offer breathtaking views. Several restaurants cater cheerfully to visitors up from the coast, some with barbecues and ethnic music

The road winds towards the centre of the island. ★★ **San Bartolomé de Tirajana** is an historic, pretty little town. Founded in the 16th century, it is the administrative centre of a region that includes the tourist developments of Maspalomas and Playa del Inglés.

San Bartolomé's principal source of income is fruit-growing. Cherries, one of the major crops, is used in the production of Guindilla, a cherry liqueur. One of the bars in the main street specialises in it.

Star Attraction
● **San Bartolomé de Tirajana**

Jeep safari
An alternative way to travel up to Fataga is in a jeep safari. Several agencies in the resorts run convoys of open-backed trucks up the steep track, usually stopping at a café and gift shop called El Mirador, with tasteless gifts and wonderful views. Lunch in Fataga is generally included. Discovery Safaris (tel: 928 775 188) throw in a free video of your adventure as well.

San Bartolomé de Tirajana

Roque Bentaiga

TWO CHURCHES

If you have time, take a stroll as far as the **Ayun-tamiento** (Town Hall), which has an attractive inner courtyard, full of flowers. There are also two churches to visit in this small town: outside the larger, neoclassical **San Bartolomé**, a bustling market is held every Sunday morning. The smaller church is **Santiago el Apóstol**, and the festival of Santiago (St James) is lavishly celebrated here on his feast day (25 July).

ROQUE BENTAIGA

From San Bartolomé, follow the signs to Tejeda – you will probably also be following a number of other four-wheel drive vehicles that have stopped for fuel in the local petrol station. Leaving the main road at the little village of Ayacata, follow signs to Bentaiga/Cueva del Rey. The first section of the track is asphalted but it soon degenerates to a gravel surface.

★★ **Roque Bentaiga** is one of the most spectacular rock monoliths in the entire range, and the journey offers a succession of dramatic panoramas. At the foot of the monolith lies the last historically documented refuge of the Guanches, a complex of caves near the hamlet of **El Roque**. First, a left fork brings you to the **Centro de Interpretación**, an archaeological museum.

Back on the main road, take the alternative route towards the small cluster of houses that makes up the hamlet, and there join the narrow path which leads first up a series of steps past the old threshing floor, then along the slope to the first of the caves. The largest, the **Cueva del Rey** (King's Cave), is a little way further on.

ROQUE NUBLO

★★ **Roque Nublo** has been visible from a great distance, but to reach it you must get back on the main road, retracing your route for a short distance before turning left at Ayacata. The Rock of Cloud rises tall and narrow like a pointing finger. Depending on the time of day, it shimmers gold or pale lilac, and viewed from the side it resembles a human face.

The best view of Roque Nublo can be had from a little parking bay to the left of the road. A *camino real*, one of the island's ancient trading routes, leads to the top; the hike, which takes about 30 minutes, is well worth the effort. Arriving on the rocky plateau you will understand why the early inhabitants of the island revered this as a holy place.

ANCIENT TRACKS

Visitors who get here early enough are usually rewarded with a clear view across the entire island. Away to the west is neighbouring Tenerife; to the north, at the foot of the mountain, you can make out La Culata with Tejeda in the distance. The *camino real* once led from La Culata across Roque Nublo and down to Ayacata. The path was just wide enough to enable two mules, laden with panniers, to pass. When the asphalt road was built at the foot of the mountain, the old track lost its significance, but has now been restored *(see box)*.

On the way back you will notice a rock rising out of the ridge on the eastern side. Using a little imagination it could be seen as a praying monk, which explains the name **El Fraile** (The Monk).

Star Attraction
● **Roque Bentaiga**
● **Roque Nublo**

Walking information
Local authorities are keen to promote responsible use of the *caminos reales*. For information about those around Roque Nublo and Roque Bentaiga, contact the Ayuntamiento (Town Hall) in Tejeda at Plaza del Socorro, tel: 928 666 001, fax: 928 666 252. They can give details of the altitudes, types of terrain, and the estimated time a hike will take. The Patronato de Turismo in Las Palmas (tel: 928 219 600) also produces a helpful series of maps and leaflets. They are in Spanish, but the basic information is clear.

The mountainous heartlands

Map on page 88

Well of snow
Pico de las Nieves means Peak of the Snows, but it has another name – Pozo de las Nieves. *Pozo* means well. There was a well here which became filled with compressed snow in winter. The ice remained frozen until summer and could then be transported to hospitals in Las Palmas where it was used for cooling patients during operations.

Café break in the hills

PICO DE LAS NIEVES

Passing the dam called Presa de los Hornos, the route continues towards Cruz de Tejeda, past the Centro de Interpretación Degollada de Bercerra, an information centre. About 3km (2 miles) after the reservoir, a road on the right leads to ★ **Pico de las Nieves**, the highest peak on the island, crowned by a radar station and TV transmitter.

The road passes round a prohibited, military area and thence to an observation point from which there is a superb view of Roque Nublo. A second viewing point a little further on provides more splendid views of the surrounding hills, often as far as Mount Teide on Tenerife – assuming that Pico de las Nieves is not shrouded in the dense clouds brought in by the trade winds.

CRUZ DE TEJEDA

The main roads in the centre of the island meet at the ★ **Cruz de Tejeda**, a stone cross marking the top of the 1,580-m (5,184-ft) pass. This is one of the regular stops for coach tours so there is a bustle of commercial activity. Two reliable restaurants, El Refugio and Yolanda, cater to visitors. There is also a *parador*, the **Hostería de Cruz de Tejeda**, designed in the 1930s in typical Canarian style by Néstor Martín-Fernández de la Torre *(see page 38),* but it has been under renovation for some time and, in the spring of 2003, was not near to completion. To find out if it has re-opened when you visit, check with the tourist office in Las Palmas (tel: 928 219 600).

The road continues in the direction of Artenara. It lives up to its reputation as one of the most beautiful, but also one of the most dangerous, stretches on the island. Visitors suffering from vertigo should refrain from looking over the edge.

ARTENARA

★★ **Artenara**, at an altitude of 1,270m (4,167ft), is the highest village on Gran Canaria. It also has a further attraction: almost all the houses in the village and the surrounding hamlets are built into the solid rock. There is even a **cave church**, recognised by a bell above the entrance. Some of the cave houses in the village are not immediately recognisable as such because they have ordinary, painted façades. The inhabitants also have most modern amenities.

What it must be like to live in such a house can be imagined after a visit to **Mesón la Silla** cave restaurant. It lies below the village centre, where house No 9 marks the position of the long entrance tunnel. From the sunny terrace in front there is a magnificent view of Roque Bentaiga and Roque Nublo. The local dishes produced in the kitchen are substantial and good.

PINAR DE TAMADABA

From Artenara it is worth making a detour to the ★★ **Pinar de Tamadaba**, the only forest in the central massif and the finest on Gran Canaria. Large sections have been replanted with Canary pines. Blackened tree trunks reveal that forest fires are a perpetual problem, but the Canary pine, seems to cope much better than other species. Many of the tall, slender trees have long lichens hanging from them.

Returning along the same road and driving back through Artenara, the route leaves the main road to follow a narrow, minor road to **Tejeda**. The vil-

Star Attractions
● **Artenara**
● **Pinar de Tamadaba**

Below: Artenara cave restaurant
Bottom: Tejeda church

Map on page 88

Dry village

There are five reservoirs within the Tejeda community boundaries – Los Hornos, Soria, Parlillo, Cueva de las Niñas and Caidero de la Niña. Unfortunately, the water they contain does not belong to nor benefit the village: instead, it is piped to Las Palmas, with the result that there is very little drinking water in Tejeda during the dry summer months.

lage is set in a stunning location at an altitude of 1,050m (3,444ft). The main street is laid out like a promenade and provides fantastic views of Roque Bentaiga. Just behind the plaza and the church, narrow, crooked alleys wind through the oldest part of the village. Cracks are appearing in the idyll, however: terraced farming is no longer viable and most inhabitants now commute to work in one of the main centres.

SANTA LUCIA

Our route returns now to San Bartolomé de Tirajana, but instead of continuing straight down the Barranco de Fataga towards the coast, turn left just after the village along the GC-655 towards ★★ **Santa Lucía**. This pretty village nestles between flower gardens and palm trees in the upper region of the **Barranco de Tirajana**, in one of the most attractive regions on the entire island.

The feathery crowns of the palm trees form an attractive contrast to the stark rocks of the surroundings. The whitewashed houses of the village are clustered around the prominent domed church, which has a distinctly mosque-like appearance and a double bell tower.

Santa Lucía

RESTAURANT HAO

Don't miss the opportunity of stopping at ★ **Restaurant Hao**, one of the most popular local eating places, with planked tables and wooden stools. It is worth visiting for several reasons, among them the cheerful atmosphere and the local speciality of roast kid cooked on the grill (*cabrito*, but also called *baifo*).

There is also a small museum, the **Museo Castillo de la Fortaleza** (open daily 9am–5pm), run by the owner. Designed like a medieval castle, it houses his many finds including bones, Guanche mummies, tools, pottery and clothing from the pre-Spanish period. One of the special treasures of the private collection is a Roman amphora, dating from the 3rd century AD and found on the sea bed off Lanzarote. Don't be put off if the restaurant is crowded; customers don't usually wait long to get served. It is worth stopping just for a drink under the pergola. If you're not driving you could try the locally distilled rum, honey and lemon liqueur *Mejunje*.

FORTALEZA GRANDE

Some 3km (2 miles) south of Santa Lucía, on the west side of the C815, is **Fortaleza Grande** itself, a rock formation shaped like a castle. Historical documents tell us that it was one of the last refuges of the Guanches. From the road you can make out numerous caves and rock paths; there is a footpath, but it is advisable to explore the area only if you have appropriate equipment. Minimum requirements are stout shoes and a torch.

To the Guanches this was a sacred spot, and in April 1483, during the last days of the Spanish conquest, some 1,600 men, women and children entrenched themselves here until persuaded to surrender by their former chief, Tenesor Semidan *(see page 24)*, who had reluctantly converted to Christianity. The event is still commemorated every year on 29 April.

The road descends from here through countless bends to the plain on the eastern side of the island, from where the motorway leads back to the starting point of the route.

Below: Santa Lucía's archaeological museum, in a mock castle
Bottom: a parting shot

Artistic Origins

Little remains today of the original art and culture of the Canary Islands. The first settlers are usually known as the Guanches; in fact, this was the name of the early inhabitants of Tenerife, but is widely used to refer to the aboriginal people of all the islands. They left us their pottery skills and farming techniques, while the Spanish conquerors brought Flemish paintings, and the work of Moorish stonemasons and Andalusian carpenters. Folk music which originated in South America bears witness to the (much later) influence of returning emigrants on their homeland.

ANCIENT DESIGNS

Gran Canaria is dotted with evidence of a flourishing pre-Hispanic culture. There are elaborate systems of cave dwellings, such as those in La Atalaya, which are believed to have been almost continuously inhabited since Guanche times. The Cenobio de Valerón *(see page 53)*, near Moya in the north-west of the island, was a large grain store; and there are a number of cult sites including an important one, at Montaña de las Cuatro Puertas *(see page 67)*.

Apart from ceramics *(see page 102)*, rock drawings are all that remain of the indigenous people's art. They have been found on the island in the form of geometric patterns, although the Cueva Pintada in Gáldar *(see page 55)* is the only place where the geometrical patterns decorating the cave walls were painted in colour.

DRY STONE WALLS

In the island interior you will often come across natural stone houses, built without the use of mortar. Two concave walls are built facing each other, and the spaces in between the stones are filled in with detritus. Since winter frosts are unknown in Gran Canaria, such walls can last for centuries. It is possible that the original islanders built their homes in this way, and that the style of construction has been preserved until the present day.

Domestic artefacts
Some of the Guanches' domestic and agricultural tools have been discovered at various sites. Stone and bone were used for needles and fish-hooks, basalt for heavy knives and chopping implements and obsidian for finer knives. Containers were made from wood, leather, pottery and basketry. The dry climate has preserved some of them very well, as can be seen in the Museo Canario in Las Palmas.

Opposite: Casa de Colón, Las Palmas
Bottom: stone carving, Museo Canario

Canarian architecture

The best places to see typical Canary Island architecture are in the Vegueta district of Las Palmas and in Teror. The Calle de los Balcones in Vegueta has some wonderful examples of carved balconies and ornate doorways. The Casa de Colón and the Museo Pérez Galdós are two museums that allow you to admire the interior of such buildings.

Teror has many examples of domestic buildings in the Canarian style, mostly in the street that leads to the church. The Museo de los Patrones, near the church, is an excellent place to see inside one of them, furnished throughout in 17th-century style.

Traditional-style balcony

Architecture

The Moors bequeathed to the Canary Islands, as to Andalusia, the style known as *mudéjar*. When the Arabs were expelled from Spain, those who remained behind converted to Catholicism, but continued to decorate their buildings with geometrically-based designs. Islam forbids artists to use representations of living creatures in their ornamentation, and even after conversion they continued to seek inspiration in imaginative forms, for which plants and geometric patterns formed the basis.

On the Canary Islands, many churches and palaces have wooden roofs built in *mudéjar* style. On doorways and window supports, too, you will often find carved *mudéjar* elements.

The master builders responsible for many of the magnificent 16th-century buildings still standing today, and which are now regarded as typically Canarian in style, came from Andalusia. Behind the enclosed, ornately-carved Moorish balconies, the wives and daughters of prosperous citizens were forced to remain partially hidden from view.

The ornately carved doorways, gleaming tiles and shady courtyards, often centred on a fountain, also show distinct Moorish influences.

Art and Sculpture

Geographical isolation and centuries of poverty explain why the Canary Islands has little to show in the way of indigenous artistic creativity. Many churches and palaces on the island contain paintings and altar pieces by 16th- and 17th-century Flemish masters. At the time, the Netherlands formed part of the Spanish empire and local merchants, having risen to prosperity as a result of the sugar trade, could afford to import the work of the leading artists of the time – in fact, it was a matter of some prestige to do so.

The most famous 18th-century Canarian sculptor was José Luján Pérez, who was born in Santa María de Guía and whose work adorns the

Catedral de Santa Ana and many other buildings in Las Palmas, and in the church in Guía.

NESTOR

Néstor Martín-Fernández de la Torre (1887–1938) was Gran Canaria's most famous painter. He was born in Las Palmas, where there is a museum dedicated to him in the Pueblo Canario *(see page 38)*. Néstor, as he is always known, was a leading Modernist, who worked for most of his life in Paris, Madrid and Barcelona. Towards the end of his life he became very conscious of his island roots and returned home, where he painted a series called *Visiones de Gran Canaria*.

CESAR MANRIQUE

The best-known 20th-century Canarian artist – and the only one apart from Néstor to achieve world fame – was César Manrique (1920–92), a native of Lanzarote. His international reputation rests not only on his paintings and sculptures but on his work as an environmentalist. He fought tirelessly to preserve the islands from thoughtless and ill-planned building schemes. There is not much of his work to be seen in Gran Canaria, but in Lanzarote it adorns parks, gardens and roundabouts as well as being displayed in galleries.

Below: Poema de la Tierra *by Néstor*
Bottom: Manrique's vision of the islands

Handicrafts

The legacy of the Guanches can clearly be seen in the local ceramics. The pots, which were used for domestic and ritual purposes, were formed without a potter's wheel and thus have no 'foot'. They were made by placing strips of clay on top of each other and were decorated with fine motifs. The most typical examples are brick-red with black geometric designs.

The art of ceramics was traditionally practised by women, and reveals definite similarities with the pottery of North Africa – one of the pieces of evidence pointing to a link between the North African Berbers and the Guanches. Terracotta stamps *(pintaderas)*, which also had geometric designs, were used to print patterns on cloth, and it is believed they may also have been used as security seals on grain stores.

Some fine examples of Guanche pottery can be seen in the Museo Canario in Las Palmas, and authentic-looking copies are made and sold in La Atalaya and elsewhere.

Literature

Gran Canaria produced only one writer whose name would be internationally recognised. He was Benito Pérez Galdós (1843–1920), one of Spain's greatest novelists and dramatists – some

Below: lacemaking, Ingenio
Bottom: tableware, Puerto de Mogán

say *the* greatest after Cervantes – who was born in Las Palmas, where his home is now a museum *(see page 34)*. He spent most of his life on the mainland, in Madrid and Santander, but returned to his homeland in 1914. His work had great social and cultural significance in its time, and some believe he was only denied the Nobel Prize for political reasons, due to his outspoken republican and anti-clerical views. He is still widely read today, and one of his novels, *Nazarín*, was filmed during the 1960s by the subversive master of Spanish film, Luís Buñuel.

Festivals and Folklore

FIESTAS

On Gran Canaria each town and village celebrates an annual fiesta, mostly to mark the name day of the patron saint. There is, therefore, a religious element: often the image of the local saint, or the Virgin, is carried in procession on a decorated float to the church. But the events always include plenty of secular celebration: folkloric performances, food, drink and dancing. The latter often doesn't begin until 10pm and may go on well into the early hours of the morning.

CARNIVAL

Pre-Lent Carnival on Gran Canaria is a celebration unlike any other, and an occasion for huge and colourful celebrations. Latin American customs mix with European Christian rituals and elements of the event's pagan origins. Each year a different theme is chosen for the decorated floats and elaborate costumes of the masked revellers. Some people spend most of the year working on them. A Carnival Queen is elected to rule over the event – a much-coveted role.

Carnival precedes Lent and should end on Ash Wednesday, but it is often held when Tenerife's ends, so the dates don't clash (check with the tourist office). The biggest celebration is in Las Palmas but it also takes place in other towns.

Music
The island folk music, which can be heard at many festivals, or at performances in the Pueblo Canario in Las Palmas *(see page 38)* reveals the influence of Andalusian and North African music. Emigrants returning from South America in the 20th century brought with them the rhythms of that continent. No fiesta today would be complete without salsa, for example, which contrasts with the basic rhythms of the native music and dance.

Folk musician

> **Burying the sardine**
> One of the strangest elements of Carnival is the ceremony known as El Entierro de la Sardina – the Burial of the Sardine. To the accompaniment of loud wailing, and the beating of drums, an enormous papier-mâché fish is carried in funeral procession before being burned on a huge bonfire. Like many other strands of Carnival, this is believed to have pagan origins.

Carnival accompaniment

FESTIVAL CALENDAR

The following is a summary of the major island-wide festivals, as well as some more local ones:

January 6: *Epifanía del Señor* (Feast of the Epiphany). This is the day when Spanish children receive their Christmas presents. In Las Palmas and other places, the Three Kings *(Los Reyes)*, ride into town, sometimes on camels, throwing sweets for the children.

January 20: *San Sebastián*. The saint's day is celebrated with merrymaking in Agüimes and Guía.

February: *Fiesta de Almendros* (Almond Blossom Festival) in Tejeda and Valsequillo. The exact date depends when the blossom is at its best. There are traditional handicrafts, dancing and sports displays.

Late February/early March: Carnival celebrations are particularly riotous in Las Palmas and Playa del Inglés *(see previous page)*.

April: *Semana Santa*. The week preceding Easter is a time of solemn processions in most towns.

Mid-June: *Corpus Christi*. The streets of Vegueta and the Plaza de Santa Ana in Las Palmas, as well as the town squares in Arucas and Gáldar, are carpeted with decorative patterns of flowers, grasses and coloured sand.

June 24: *San Juan* (Feast of St John). Major celebrations in Artenara, Telde, Las Palmas and Arucas, with dancing, processions, sporting activities. Bonfires are lit on many hilltops the night before.

July 16: *Nuestra Señora del Carmen*, the patron saint of fishermen, is honoured on this and surrounding days. Statues of the Virgin are taken out to sea in processions of beautifully decorated boats, and there are plenty of festivities on land. Celebrations are held in all ports but are especially colourful in Arguineguín and Puerto de Mogán.

August 4: *Bajada de la Rama* (Bringing down the Branches) is held in Agaete and the neighbouring port of Puerto de las Nieves. The festival is pagan in origin and symbolises prayers for fertility and rain. The villagers carry branches from the mountains to the sea and whip the waves.

September 8: *Virgen del Pino*. Important festival in Teror to which people come from all over the island. A mixture of pious religious processions and secular merrymaking.

September 11: *Fiesta del Charco* (Festival of the Lagoon) in Puerto de la Aldea, near San Nicolás. Participants try to catch fish with their hands, and throw each other into the water.

Second Saturday in October: *Fiestas de la Naval* (Festival of the Sea). Celebrates the 1595 victory of the Armada over the English. Maritime processions in Las Palmas and other ports.

LUCHA CANARIA

Canary Islands wrestling was practised by the indigenous island people. Contests are held in a sandy ring. Two teams of twelve wrestlers take it in turns to face a member of the opposing team. All parts of the body may be used except the feet, and the aim is to throw the opponent to the floor. After a maximum of three rounds the winner is the team which has lost the fewest wrestlers. *Lucha canaria* is the most popular traditional sport on the islands and can be seen at local fiestas. Competitions also take place in Las Palmas in the Estadio López Socas and in Gáldar.

Juego del palo (stick fighting) is an ancient rural sport now practised at fiestas. The object is to move the body as little as possible while attacking and fending off the blows of an opponent.

Below: lucha canaria, or local wrestling
Bottom: Baja de la Rama

FOOD AND DRINK

Gran Canaria can offer culinary delights to satisfy every taste: from gourmet restaurants to simple country inns, you will find good places to eat on every corner. Of course there are establishments – mostly in the south – where visitors will find such familiar delights as fish and chips, burgers and spaghetti bolognese. Tracking down a little fishermen's bar or a *parilla,* with typical local specialities, outside the main tourist centres, is a little more difficult. Such restaurants seldom have a menu, although there is often a slate listing the dishes available that day (remember to take a dictionary).

WHERE TO EAT

Where can you buy what? A *kiosco* sells not newspapers but coffee, refreshments and perhaps, at most, a *bocadillo*, a sandwich. Coffee is available on the Canary Islands in three variations, which are drunk at any time of day: *café solo* (espresso), *cortado* (espresso with a little milk or cream) and *café con leche* (espresso with lots of milk). A *kiosco* will be found on almost every square, even in small villages, and serves as a popular meeting place among local people at any time of day or night.

The same applies to bars, which have nothing to do with nightlife. They are found in every village street and in all districts of a town. Closing time is usually 11pm but may be much later in Las Palmas and the resorts. They serve all kinds of drinks, but no food except, sometimes, tapas – the little snacks that can usually be chosen from a display in a glass case or laid out on the bar. *Tapa* is the Spanish word for lid, and the name derives from the cus-

tom of placing a small plate on top of a wine glass to keep away flies. Barkeepers soon had the idea of putting a small appetiser on the plate, and the tradition of tapas was born.

A *parilla* (grill) is a rustic inn with wooden tables and benches. The menu consists principally of grilled meat and occasionally fish. The best example of a *parilla* is the Hao in Santa Lucía (*see page 96*). The food is quite simple and the prices modest.

SPECIALITIES

Don't miss the local specialities such as fresh fish, which is certain to have been landed at the nearest port that very morning. Local people prefer *cherne, vieja* and *sama* – bass, parrot fish and sea bream, respectively, as well as the ubiquitous salt cod *(bacalao)*. But in fact a true fishermen's tavern will serve fish and seafood of all kinds, although not every species is available all year round. In season you will find *gambas* (prawns)*, pulpo* (octopus)*, calamares* (squid)*, merluza* (hake)*, bonito* (a variety of tuna) and *sardinas* (sardines).

The fish is often served with *papas arrugadas*, 'wrinkled' potatoes. The

> **Breakfast on the island**
> As in mainland Spain, the people of the Canary Islands don't take breakfast seriously – coffee or thick chocolate and fresh bread or *churros* (a kind of sausage-shaped doughnut) are usually all that is on offer. This does not apply to hotels catering for tourists, however – the only ones where breakfast is usually included in the room price. These will usually serve a buffet-style breakfast that will include fresh fruit, sometimes eggs, ham or cheese, as well as rolls or croissants.

Left: café in Parque San Telmo

method originated with fishermen who used to boil the well-scrubbed, unpeeled potatoes in seawater until the water evaporated and formed a salt crust round the wrinkled potatoes. The skin, with its salt crust, is also eaten. You won't find them cooked in sea-water these days, but they crop up on most menus.

Fish and potatoes are usually accompanied by *mojo verde*, a green sauce made with oil, vinegar, garlic, coriander and parsley; meat is often served with *mojo rojo*, a spicier, reddish version prepared with chilli and peppers.

Among meat dishes you will find *carne de cerdo* or *chuletas* – grilled pork escalope or chops. Also popular are *cabrito*, kid – sometimes called *baifo* – and *conejo*, rabbit, both of which may be served *en salmorejo* (in a herb and garlic marinade).

Other specialities include a range of filling soups and stews: *ropa vieja* (literally, old clothes) is a thick soup based on meat and chick-peas; *sancocho* is made of salted fish, usually cod, potatoes and herbs and served with *mojo verde*; *puchero*, the most famous of the traditional stews, includes meat, pumpkin and a variety of vegetables. In a typical *parilla* they will all be served with *gofio*, the Canaries' most famous speciality.

Economical menus

Many restaurants in the southern resorts, and those in the area of Las Palmas used to catering to visitors, will have a set menu – the *menú del día* – offering three courses and often including wine or water. The choice on these menus is not wide – the first course is often a salad or soup, the third one usually fruit or ice cream, but they are a very economical way to eat. Many places only offer this menu at lunchtime, however, which for most islanders is the main meal of the day.

GOFIO

Made of wheat, barley or a mixture of the two, *gofio* was the staple food of the original inhabitants of the Canary Islands. If no cereals were available it was made with the roots of ferns. When the islands were colonised, the conquerors took over this wholefood dish, and it still forms an essential part of the local diet today.

To prepare *gofio*, the cereal is roasted before being ground into flour. When this process is complete, the flour should on no account be cooked any more because it would turn solid and be impossible to blend with liquid. It can be made into a paste with water or milk and kneaded into balls together with sugar, honey, almonds, bananas, oranges or even cheese. It is stirred into children's milk and used to thicken sauces. It is also blended with fish stock to make a thick soup called *gofio escaldado*.

Local people claim that eating *gofio* three times a day accounts for their remarkable physical strength. Try it as a novelty, but it isn't the tastiest thing you will find on the island.

POSTRE, CHEESE AND WINE

Favourite desserts *(postres)*, include the delicious *bienmesabe*, a highly calorific dish prepared from almonds and honey; crème caramel, sometimes known here, as in the rest of Spain, as 'flan'; and *queso blanco*, a piquant goat's cheese. Particularly recommended is *queso de flor*, a sweetish cheese from Santa María de Guía, made of cow's and sheep's milk with the addition of thistle-flower juice.

In addition to the strongly flavoured, sometimes rather heavy, local wines, almost all of which are produced on neighbouring islands, the Canary Islands are known for a light beer which is produced locally under the brand names Dorada and Tropical.

RESTAURANT SELECTION

The following are suggestions for just a few of the more popular spots on the island. You may be surprised to see that some of them close for a month in summer. The following categories have been used, for a 3-course meal for one with house wine: €€€ = over €35; €€ = €20–35; € =below €20.

Las Palmas

Amaiur, Pérez Galdós 2,tel: 928 370 717. Imaginative, well-presented dishes from the Basque country, a region that is known for its good food. Closed Sunday. €€€.

Casa Julio, La Naval 132, Puerto de la Luz, tel: 928 460 139. Specialises in excellent fish and seafood with Basque and Gallego influences. Closed Sunday. €€€.

El Cerdo Que Ríe, Paseo de las Canteras 31, tel: 928 271 731. Extremely popular, The Laughing Pig has been going since the 1960s; has a large, Scandinavian influenced menu. €€.

El Cucharón, Reloj 2, tel: 928 333 296. In Vegueta. Elegant décor and authentic island food. Closed Saturday lunchtime, all day Sunday and mid-August to mid-September. €€.

Dedo de Dios restaurant, Puerto de las Nieves

El Gallo Rojo, Paseo de las Canteras 35, tel: 928 271 731. Sister of The Laughing Pig; similar menu and prices, but a bit quieter. Closed in August. €€.

El Herreño, Medizábal 5, tel: 928 310 513. Close to the Vegueta market, this restaurant serves hearty, simple food from El Hierro island, in a friendly atmosphere. €€.

O'Sole Mio, Plaza Cairasco 3, tel: 928 383 746. Pizza, pasta served in a large dining room and at tables out in the little square. €.

El Padrino, Jesús Nazareno 1, tel: 928 462 094. This fish restaurant on La Isleta is famous not only for its seafood, but also for marvellous views. Particularly recommended for warm summer evenings and Sunday lunch. Reached by Bus No 41 from Parque Santa Catalina, but you may need a taxi back at night. €€.

Hipócrates, Colón 4, Vegueta, tel: 928 311 171. Friendly vegetarian restaurant right opposite Casa de Colón. Good salads and *gazpacho*. Closed Monday lunch and Sunday evening. €

Pepe El Breca, Prudencia Morales 16, tel: 928 468 791. Excellent, long established fish restaurant, near the beach. Let the staff advise you what to eat. Booking advisable. €€–€€€.

El Pescador, Marina 8, tel: 928 330 432. It's in the San Cristobál fishermen's quarter, and the name means The Fisherman, so the wide selection of fresh fish is to be expected. Caters to a pleasantly varied crowd – locals, tourists and business lunchers. €€.

El Rincón Criollo, Miguel Rosas 3, tel: 928 265 850. Small, cheerful Cuban restaurant specialising in creole dishes. Closed Sunday. €€.

El Rincón de Pepe Luján, Joaquín Costa 25, tel: 928 263 733. Old established venue and very popular; there's always a welcoming atmosphere. Closed Sunday. €€.

Tesoro Chino, Gravina 50, tel: 928 226 159. Near the main shopping dis-

---

☀ Hotel restaurants
Some of the better hotels have restaurants that are open to non-residents. The Reina Isabel, tel: 928 260 100 (€€€) and Los Bardinos, tel: 928 266 100 (€€), both close to the beach in Las Palmas, have excellent restaurants with splendid views.

---

trict, this Chinese restaurant is a great local favourite. €€.

Agüimes
La Oroval, Progreso 12 , tel: 928 78 50 03. One of the high-quality Hecansa chain. Housed in the Casa de los Camellos rural hotel, in an attractive colonial-style building, it serves traditional Canarian dishes, well-presented. Try the tiny *chorizos* in cider sauce. €€.

Artenara
Mesón La Silla, tel: 928 666 108. This is the famous cave restaurant, with spectacular views from its sunny terrace, and kitchens cut in the rock. Typical meat dishes with *mojo* sauce. Closes at sunset. €.

Maspalomas
Amaiur, Avenida T. Neckermann (opposite the golf club), tel: 928 764 414. Sister restaurant to the one in Las Palmas, with the same attention to quality and detail, albeit a slightly more international menu. €€–€€€.

La Foresta, Maspalomas Oasis Hotel, Avenida del Oasis, tel: 928 141 448. If you feel like splashing out, the food in this luxury hotel is renowned and the surroundings are stunning. €€€.

Pepe El Breca II, Carretera de Fataga, tel: 928 772 637. Run by the daughter of Pepe El Breca in Las Palmas. The sea bass baked in salt is excellent. Slightly off the beaten track, but well worth it. €€.

Playa del Inglés
Carlos V, Centro Comercial Citá, tel: 928 760 221. Excellent grilled meat dominates a long, varied menu. €€.

Las Cumbres, Avenida de Tirajana 11, tel: 928 760 941. Specialises in lamb, slowly roasted in the Spanish-style. Closed Tues and all May. €€.

La Toja, Edificio Barbados, Avenida de Tirajana 17, tel: 928 761 196. Small and pleasant; specialises in Galician food with original sauces. Closed in June. €€€.

Tenderete II, Edificio Aloe, Avenida de Tirajana 15, tel: 928 761 460. Local fish and meat dishes, attractive, rural décor. Reservations advisable. €€€.

Puerto de Mogán
La Bodeguilla Juananá, Puerto Deportivo, tel: 928 565 044. Tucked in a little square just off the quayside, this tiny place is festooned with hams and peppers and specialises in Canarian food, including island cheeses and wines. €€.

La Cofradía, Dársena Exterior s/n, tel: 928 565 321. Local favourite on the fishermen's quay, where the fish is reliably good and fresh. €€.

Santa Brígida

Mano de Hierro, Carretera del Centro Km 15, tel: 928 64 0 388. Said to be one of the best German restaurants in Spain and very popular with people from Las Palmas. Open for lunch Tues–Sun, dinner Fri–Sat. **€**.

Bistro Monte, Carretera del Centro 125, tel: 928 351 744. Formal dining room and attractive terrace and patio. Up-market Canarian dishes and local wines. Caters to a well-heeled Las Palmas crowd at weekends. **€€**.

Satautey, Real de Coello 2, tel: 928 35 53 30. Another one in the Hecansa chain, this time in the Hotel Escuela Santa Brígida. Interesting and well-presented dishes in a huge, rather forbidding, dining room. **€€€**.

Santa Lucía

Restaurant Hao, Tomás Arroyo Cardosa, tel: 928 798 007. Typical *parilla* on the main road. Serves fresh kid (*cabrito*) from the grill. Long plank tables encourage conversation. There is also a small archeological museum (*see page 96*). **€**.

Tafira Alta

La Masia de Canarias, Murillo 36, tel: 928 350 120. Excellent food in pleasant surroundings. The steaks and the salad roquefort are particularly recommended. Booking advisable at weekends. **€€€**.

Tejeda

El Refugio, Cruz de Tejeda, tel: 928 666 188. Eat indoors or outside on the roof terrace. Roast meats, stews and good salads; very good value. Brilliant views across the mountains. **€**.

Telde

La Posada, Navarra 6 tel: 928 693 623. Small, friendly place with rustic decor and good food, especially fish, both local and international. **€€€**.

Nightlife

Discos, clubs and bars open and close and fall in and out of favour very rapidly, as they do anywhere else, so the following is only a guide. Be warned that very little happens before midnight. In Las Palmas, most people head towards Plaza de España in the Mesa y López district for late-night entertainment. Heineken, at No 7, where the jukebox plays mainly golden oldies, is an old favourite here. A newer neighbour is El Cinco (tel: 928 273 266), another terraced bar in the square. La Floridita (Remedios, near the Plaza Hurtado de Mendoza; tel: 928 431 740), an Havana-style nightclub, is popular, but don't get going until late. Zorba's and Kapital, both in Luís Morote (Santa Catalina district) are bars with music and a long record for crowd-pulling.

Around 2am, those in the know move towards the port. Pacha (Simón Bolívar 3, tel: 928 271 684) has a tiny dance floor in front of a giant video screen, but you can just have a relatively quiet drink on the outside terrace.

Playa del Inglés and Maspalomas have so many bars and discos it would be impossible to name them, but there is plenty of information once you are there. All the commercial centres have their hot spots. Among the Kasbah's biggest, and most lasting, are El Garaje and Fantasy Island, while in Plaza de Maspalomas, Pacha and Chic are the places to be.

Casinos

There are two casinos on the island; one is in the luxurious Hotel Santa Catalina in Las Palmas (tel: 928 233 908); the other is the Gran Canaria Casino (tel: 928 762 724) in Hotel Meliá Tamarindos in San Agustín.

Classical music

If you want to hear classical music while you are in Las Palmas, try the Auditorio Alfredo Klaus at the far end of Playa de las Canteras (tel: 928 491 770), which presents excellent concerts and recitals; or the new Teatro Cuyás, Calle Viera y Clavijo s/n, Triana (tel: 928 432 180), which also hosts world music and theatre.

ACTIVE HOLIDAYS

WALKING

Gran Canaria offers plenty of opportunities for walks to suit people of every interest and physical condition. You can wander for weeks unaccompanied through the dense vegetation of the *barrancos*, or follow a guide along wide, easy paths. For some time work has been in progress to repair, signpost and maintain the *caminos reales*, the ancient trading routes. These routes now allow access to parts of the interior that were inaccessible.

A guidebook to these paths can be purchased in the bookshop of the Cabildo de Gran Canario, Cano 24, Las Palmas. Or contact the Patronato de Turismo, León y Castillo 17, Las Palmas, tel: 928 219 600, fax: 928 219 601, www.grancanria.com or RETUR (Asociación de Turismo Rural), Lourdes 2, Vega de San Mateo, tel: 928 661 668, fax: 928 661 560.

Remember that even easy day trips require a certain amount of preparation. Never set out on an excursion alone, and don't rely absolutely on a map. It is advisable to wear ankle-high walking boots, to set off before lunch

and to always carry sunblock, a hat, something warm for higher altitudes, and some waterproof clothing.

Guided walks for groups are offered by a number of hotels and travel agencies. Ask local tourist offices for details of reputable ones. A central organisation is **Grupo Montañero Gran Canaria**, 15 de noviembre 6, Las Palmas, tel: 928 249 2292. **Caminos de Herradura**, Drago 11, Agüimes, tel: 928 789 099, e-mail caminoherradura@terra.es, organise walks in the Barranco de Guayadeque and have extensive local knowledge.

GOLF

There are three **golf courses** in the north of the island and three in the south. The major ones are the **Real Club de Golf de Las Palmas**, Santa Brígida, tel: 928 350 104; 18 holes, course 5.7km (3½ miles), founded by British expatriates in 1891 and the oldest in Spain; **Maspalomas Golf Club**, Avenida Neckermann s/n, tel: 928 762 581; 18 holes, course 3.2km (2 miles), which has also been operating for some years; and the **Salobre Golf Club**, Autopista GC1, Km 53 between Maspalomas and Puerto de Mogán, tel: 928 010 103 for more details.

The Maspalomas golf club has a 3.2-km (2-mile) course

RIDING

The **Real Club de Golf at Santa Brígida** (tel: 928 351 050) also has a riding school. Riding lessons and trekking can be organised at **Rancho Park**, Playa del Inglés, on the road to Palmitos Park, tel: 928 766 874.

CYCLING

Four cycling routes have been established by the Maspalomas local authority. They range in length from 13km (8 miles) to 100km (62 miles), some on (relatively) flat terrain, some steeply uphill. For details of routes and degrees of difficulty, tel/fax: 928 773 326. There are also several local agencies that rent bikes and organise excursions. **Free Motion**, Avda Alféreces Provisonales, Playa del Inglés, tel: 928 777 470 rents mountain bikes, as well as organising quad safaris.

TENNIS

Las Palmas has the **Club de Tenis Gran Canaria**, Beethoven 4, tel: 928. 243 434. Nearly all the big resort hotels have tennis courts. There is also the **Club de Tenis Dunaflor**, Campo Internacional, Maspalomas, tel: 928 767 447, and several others.

WATERSPORTS

In **Las Palmas** there are two marinas of interest: the **Real Club Náutico**, León y Castillo 308, tel: 928 234 566; and the **Real Club Victoria**, Paseo de las Canteras 4, tel: 928 460 630.

For diving in Las Palmas, contact **Buceo Canarias**, Bernardo de la Torre 56–58, tel: 928 262 786; or the **Club Deportivo Tacoronte**, Pío XII 67, tel: 928 246 810.

For sailors in the **south**, there's **Pasito Blanco Yacht Club**, Carretera Central Km 60, tel: 928 142 194; the **Escuela Deportiva Náutica Anfi del Mar**, Playa Barranco de la Vega, Mogán, tel: 928 150 798; and the

Club Regatas Suroeste Mogán, Arguineguín, tel: 928 560 772.

For water skiing, try the **Water Ski School**, Puerto Rico, tel: 928 561 620 or **Molina Sport**, Playa Anfi del Mar, tel: 928 151 417.

A recommended diving school is the **Centro Turístico de Submarinismo Sun Sub**, Hotel Buenaventura Playa, Plaza de Ansit s/n, Playa del Inglés, tel: 928 778 165.

For surfing/windsurfing try the **Club Mistral Canarias**, Urb. Bahía Feliz, Carretera General del sur Km 44, tel: 928 157 158, or the **F2 Surfcenter Dunkerbeck**, Plaza de Hibiscus 2, Playa del Águila, tel: 928 762

Fishing trips

Conditions in Gran Canaria are excellent for deep-sea game fishing, with tuna, bonito and marlin prevalent. The marinas at Pasito Blanco, Puerto Rico and Puerto de Mogán all offer sports fishing trips on such boats as *Catfish* (tel: 928 561 146), *Shellfish* (tel: 928 565 258), *White Striker* (tel: 928 735 013) and *Blue Marlin* (mobile: 607 626 237). The *Crucero* (tel: 928 268 280), at the entrance to the Puerto Rico marina, offers a shark fishing trip with breakfast and lunch included, and a stop at a small cove.

958, run by world champion Björn Dunkerbeck. There are many others, all widely advertised in the resorts. PWA Grand Slam championships are held in Bahía de Pozo Izquierdo on the east coast, near Arinaga.

FLYING AND PARACHUTING

If you want to try flying or parachuting contact the **Escuela Canaria de Parapente**, Club Siroco, Las Palmas tel: 928 267 520 (courses from beginners to advanced) or the **Aeroclub de Gran Canaria**, Carretera a Mogán 46, Mogán, tel: 928 762 447.

PRACTICAL INFORMATION

Getting There

Gran Canaria can be reached by sea or by air. The average flight time from England is four hours; by ship, the voyage from the port of Cádiz on the Spanish mainland takes between two and two and a half days.

BY AIR

The Spanish national airline, Iberia, flies from London to Las Palmas, and it is also possible to fly from international airports around the world to Madrid, and pick up a domestic flight there. However, there are numerous flights to Las Palmas by the budget airlines from most airports in the UK and from other European cities all year round. You can get good flight-only deals (check the web and advertisements in travel sections of Sunday newspapers), as well as packages that include accommodation.

Gran Canaria's international airport, Aeopuerto de Gando (tel: 928 579 138/579 094) has been extended to accommodate visitors travelling on to Lanzarote, Tenerife or Fuerteven-

Drivers in Las Palmas
are well directed

tura. It is situated 20km (12 miles) south of Las Palmas. There is no shuttle bus service from the airport. Visitors can either get a half-hourly bus (No 60) to Parque San Telmo or Parque Santa Catalina, both in the centre of Las Palmas (around €1.70) or take a taxi (about €20).

Travelling south, most visitors are met by a tour operator's representative and taken by coach. If you are not on a package tour you can get a No 60 bus to Maspalomas or No 66 to Playa del Inglés, where it is possible to change for services to Puerto Rico and Puerto de Mogán. Otherwise you must get a taxi. Always check charges for out-of-town trips before starting a journey.

BY SEA

The Trasmediterránea ferry company runs a weekly service from Cádiz to Las Palmas. As mentioned above, this takes at least two days so is normally only used by those travelling extensively in Spain. For details, tel: 902 454 645; or contact the website www.trasmediterranea.es

ISLAND-HOPPING

Trasmediterránea operates jetfoils to Tenerife from Las Palmas, a trip that

takes 80 minutes. The same company runs ferries to Fuerteventura and Lanzarote (tel: 902 454 645 for general information; 928 273 884 for jetfoils, 928 474 474 for ferries; www.trasmediterranea.es). The Fred Olsen Shipping Line (tel: 928 495 040; www.fredolsen.es; e-mail: reservas@fredolsen.es) also runs ferries from Las Palmas to Fuerteventura and Lanzarote, and has six departures a day from Puerto de las Nieves (near Agaete) to Tenerife (free bus from Parque Santa Catalina). Naviera Armas (tel: 928 300 600 or 928 227 311; www.naviera-armas.com) also has regular services to Tenerife (crossing time about two hours).

There is an inter-island flight service operated by Binter Airlines (tel: 902 391 392/928 579 433; www.bintercanarias.es for information, or book through any travel agency).

Getting Around

BUS

There is no rail network on the islands, but there is a comprehensive network of bus routes crossing the island and linking the tourist centres. For travel in Las Palmas, the *guaguas* (buses), are cheap and reliable – journeys cost around €1. A *bono guagua* (pronounced 'bone oh wawa'), a ticket that can be used for 10 journeys, is good value and can be bought in the main bus terminal in Parque San Telmo and the newer one in Parque Santa Catalina. City buses run from dawn until about 9.30pm, and there's also an hourly night service on the major routes.

Most inter-city and long-distance buses also leave from the Parque San Telmo bus station, although some now commence their journeys at the new Santa Catalina terminal. They, too, are cheap, frequent and reliable.

They are run by the SALCAI UTINSA

company (tel: 928 360 179/928 368 335 for northern and central routes, 928 381 110/928 372 133 for southern routes). The green buses cover the south of the island and the blue and orange buses the centre and the north. Buses marked *directo* for Maspalomas (via Playa del Inglés) and Puerto Rico are extremely frequent and leave the terminals as soon as they're full.

TAXI

There is no shortage of taxis which can be flagged down as they drive past. For journeys within towns, the fare is calculated according to the meter. For longer journeys out of town the fare should be negotiated in advance. Taxis are exceptionally good value, with the longest run in Las Palmas costing only around €5.

BY CAR

The easiest way of exploring the island is to rent a car – although driving in the extremely busy streets of Las Palmas is not much fun. Parking is difficult, and the traffic police, with their notorious breakdown truck *(la grua)*, sometimes appear within minutes to tow away illegally parked cars. Tracking down a car that has 'disappeared' in this manner can cost half a day's holiday and a lot of bother, in addition

---

Taxi co-operative

In Maspalomas, taxi services are run by the Cooperativa de Taxis, Avenida Alejandro del Castillo 1, tel: 928 766 767, fax: 928 771 285. The fares are strictly controlled (the tourist office will give you a leaflet listing the charges to various popular destinations), and, as well as local services, they offer a variety of round-the-island and inland trips for prices that are fairly reasonable if several people travel together, as the charge is for the trip, not for the number of passengers.

to the hefty fine. Note that apart from the familiar international signs, no-parking zones are indicated by yellow marks on the kerb.

Outside the city, the roads are mostly of European standard, and traffic signs and rules of the road will mostly be familiar. However, a few Spanish warning signs and regulations should be noted:

carretera cortada: road blocked
ceda el paso: observe priority
desprendimentos: possible avalanches
desvio: detour.

Seat belts must be worn in Spain, as must crash helmets by motorcyclists. There are high penalties for speeding (the speed limit in built-up areas is 40kph (24mph), elsewhere 90kph (56mph) except on motorways and motorway-type roads (100kph/62mph). There are also penalties for driving a vehicle with faults, so it is advisable to examine the condition of a rented vehicle before signing the contract.

The condition of hire cars from small local companies varies considerably. To avoid problems, it is advisable to settle for one of the larger firms. Among the international companies, try:

Avis: Juan Manuel Durán González 13, Las Palmas, tel: 928 265 567; aiport: tel: 928 579 578.

Europcar: airport tel: 928 574 244; Edificio Bayuca, Alféreces Provisionales s/n, Playa del Inglés, tel: 928 765 500.

Hertz: Muelle Transbordadores, Las Palmas, tel: 928 228 846/928 228 977); airport tel: 928 579 577; Avenida Gran Canaria 14, Playa del Inglés, tel: 928 763 026; Avenida Tomás Roca Bosch 45, Puerto Rico–Mogán, tel: 928 560 012.

Among the local firms, the following are reputable and may be cheaper

Autos Beltran: Apts Solymar 4, near foot of Avenida Tirajana, Playa del Inglés, tel: 928 764 266.

Autos Canarias: Tenerife 24, Las Palmas, tel: 928 270 861.

Autos Moreno: General Vives 89, Las Palmas, tel: 928 268 480; Edificio Excelsior, Avenida de Tirajana, Playa del Inglés, tel: 928 777 385.

Autos Pérez: Hotel Sol Bardinos, Las Palmas, tel: 928 261 136, fax: 928 26 55 32; Avenida Tenerife 8, Playa del Inglés, tel: 763 616.

Orlando: Avenida Tirajana 23, Playa del Inglés, tel: 928 76 55 02.

The prices listed in brochures are not always all-inclusive. They usually include third-party insurance, but obligatory tax will be added. Fully comprehensive insurance *(todo riesgo)* usually costs extra, but is well worth having.

A small car costs about the same as anywhere else in Europe; a four-wheel drive, however, can cost more than twice as much. Automatic vehicles are hard to find. It is always advisable to go for a rental period of three days or a week as you get a much better deal.

Cheap petrol
Petrol on the Canary Islands is cheaper than just about anywhere else in Europe. Petrol stations *(gasolineras)* are mostly open until 10pm, although, like other establishments, many close during the siesta period between 2–5pm.

Remember that only people mentioned in the contract are allowed to drive the hire car. In order to rent a car you will need a credit card; even if you are able to pay by cash the company will take the card details as a form of deposit. There are also some very good deals to be had by booking in advance via the Internet, as long as you know exactly when and for how long you want a vehicle.

Facts for the Visitor

TRAVEL DOCUMENTS

Visitors from European Union countries, the Commonwealth and the United States must have a valid passport. No visa is required by nationals of the EU and US for stays of up to six months, or by Australian, Canadian or New Zealand nationals for stays of up to three months. Visitors bringing their own car will need the vehicle registration documents and insurance certificates. National driving licences are accepted in the case of visitors staying less than six months on the island.

CUSTOMS

Citizens of non-EU member states can bring 400 cigarettes, one bottle of spirits, two of wine, 50g of perfume; citizens of EU-member states have guide levels of 800 cigarettes, 10 litres of spirit and 90 litres of wine.

TOURIST INFORMATION

The state-owned **Spanish National Tourist Office** will supply information. Here some addresses:

In the UK: 22–23 Manchester Square, London W1U 3PX, tel: 020 7486 8077, fax: 020 7486 8034, brochure line: 09063 640 630, email: info.londres@tourspain.es; www.tourspain.co.uk

In the US: 666 Fifth Avenue, New York, NY 10103, tel: 212 265 8822, fax: 212 265 8864, email: nuevayork@tourspain.es

Other websites, with useful links and tourist information, you might wish to check out include: www.okspain.org, www.tourspain.es, www.red2000.com and www.grancanaria.com

LOCAL TOURIST OFFICES
Las Palmas

Patronato de Turismo, Calle León y Castillo 17, tel: 928 219 600, fax: 928 219 601.

Parque San Telmo (kiosk), tel: 928 368 335; Pueblo Canario, tel: 928 243 593.
Maspalomas

Avenida EEUU/Avenida España, tel: 928 771 550/928 762 591.
Puerto de Mogán

Lokal 329, Avenida de Mogán, tel: 928 560 029.

CURRENCY AND EXCHANGE

In 2002, the euro (EUR) became the official currency used in Spain. Notes are denominated in 5, 10, 20, 50, 100 and 500 euros; coins in 1 and 2 euros and 1, 2, 5, 10, 20 and 50 cents.

The easiest way to obtain cash is with a credit/debit card and a PIN number at a cash point *(telebanco)*. There are plenty of cash points in Las Palmas and the southern resorts, some of them housed in booths, for obvious reasons. These allow you to carry out your transactions in the language of your choice. In smaller towns you are less likely to find them but they are becoming more prevalent.

Banks change foreign currency and travellers' cheques, but charge a commission. Rates vary, so shop around. Credit cards are widely accepted, especially American Express and Visa.

TIPPING

In a restaurant or when travelling by taxi, you should round up the total sum as you would do at home. Approximately 10 percent usual. In restaurants this is sometimes added to the bill.

OPENING TIMES

Shops are generally open Monday to Friday from 9am–1pm and 5–8pm, although supermarkets and the larger stores don't close during the middle of the day and some stay open late. On Saturday, most shops are only open in the morning, although in major tourist centres they also open on Saturday afternoon and sometimes on Sunday.

From July to September, some shops and other businesses open during the morning only, but close at 2pm instead of 1pm. Special regulations apply in tourist centres allowing for extended opening hours.

Banks are open Monday to Friday 9am–2pm.

Post Offices *(correos)* are open Monday to Friday 9am–2pm, on Saturday until 1pm.

SHOPPING AND SOUVENIRS

Gran Canaria looks set to maintain its status as a Free Trade Zone for the forseeable future, so savings on items such as tobacco, spirits, perfume, cosmetics, watches, jewellery, electronic and optical equipment are still to be had, but be careful what you buy.

The shopping centres in the main tourist destinations, as well as depart-ment stores in the capital, are geared to holidaymakers and carry a wide range of goods. Bargaining is expected in markets and at street stalls.

There are a number of large shopping centres in Las Palmas. The biggest is Las Arenas (tel: 928 277 008) on Calle Paria in the north of the city, near the Auditorio Alfredo Kraus, with more than 100 shops, most of which stay open until 10pm.

La Ballena is another huge centre, in Carretera General del Norte, five minutes from the city centre. It is served by buses from Parque San Telmo, and offers free car parking.

Newest is the smaller Monopol, in Triana, but although it is right in the centre of a traditional shopping area, it doesn't seem to have taken off and many of its outlets are empty.

Along the broad Avenida de Mesa y López, as well as big department stores such as El Corte Inglés and Galerias Preciadas, there are numer-ous shops specialising in good-quality shoes and textiles.

In the narrow streets of the Santa Catalina area you will find electrical goods of every kind. Vegueta is the place to shop for souvenirs such as embroidery, basketware and pottery. Try Artesanía Canaria Tagügüys, Armas 1, not far from Casa Colón. This is also a good place to buy one of the small knives used by banana workers (*cuchillos canarios* or *naifes*). They have a wide blade and a goathorn han-dle decorated with inlaid patterns.

The FEDAC shop at Domingo J. Navarro 7, in Triana sells good qual-ity textiles, pottery, bags and scarves.

The museum shop in the Museo Canario is worth a look for replicas of items in the collection, as well as books about the islands. The Pueblo Canario souvenir shop also has some good pieces *(see page 38)*.

The Librería del Cabildo Insular (the

> **Public holidays**
>
> Spain has not only national but also regional and local public holidays. You might find all the shops in one village closed, while in the next town it is business as usual. The following holidays are observed on the island: 1 January (New Year), 6 January (Epifanía del Señor/Epiphany), 19 March (San José/St Joseph), Good Friday, Easter Sunday, 1 May (Día del Trabajo), 30 May (Día de las Canarias), mid-June (Corpus Christi), 25 July (Santiago/St James), 15 August (La Asun-ción/Assumption), 12 October (Fiesta Nacional/National Day), 1 November (Todos los Santos/All Saints'), 6 December (Constitu-ción/Constitution Day), 8 December (Inmac-ulada Concepción/Immaculate Conception), 25 December (Christmas Day).
>
> As in the rest of Spain, the habit of linking holidays with weekends by means of a day called a *puente* (bridge) is prevalent. This means, for example, that if a holiday falls on a Thursday, many people don't go back to work until the following Monday.

official government bookshop) at Calle Cano 24, Triana, is an excellent place for maps and books on the island.

Replicas of traditional Guanche pottery are sold in Calle Maestro in Santa Brígida. Made in the traditional manner without a potter's wheel and then dried in the sun, this type of pottery is not cheap but it is unique. Embroidered items can be bought in the Museo de Piedras y Artesanía in Ingenio

Ignore traders who offer ivory jewellery or leather or fur goods from endangered species. Not only will you be supporting the extermination of rare animals, but the import of such items into Europe and the US is forbidden and subject to heavy penalties.

Island markets are always worth browsing around, even if you don't buy. In the lively Mercado Municipal in Vegueta (Las Palmas), fish, meat, fruit and vegetables are piled high and there's lots of street activity. On Sunday morning there's a beautiful flower market in the Plaza de Santo Domingo in Vegueta, and a flea market *(rastro)* fills Parque Santa Catalina.

Most towns have a weekly market, when stalls are filled with handicrafts, bread and cakes, honey and local cheeses. Guía is the place for cheese *(queso de flor)*, sold by Santiago Gil Romero at Marqués de Muni 34.

In the south of the island the best market is in Puerto de Mogán on Friday morning, when traditional items as well as food and clothes are on sale around the quayside.

POSTAL SERVICES

All letters and postcards from the Canaries go by air. Mail takes at least five days to reach northern Europe. Postage stamps *(sellos)* can be purchased in post offices, tobacconists' shops *(tabacos)*, at hotel reception desks and in souvenir shops selling postcards. Spanish post-boxes are a distinctive yellow.

The main post office in Las Palmas is in Avenida 1 de Mayo 62, tel: 928 363 120; in Playa del Inglés it is in Edificio Mercurio, Avenida de Tirajana, tel: 928 762 341.

TELEPHONE

For international phone calls, it is easiest to use telephone booths called *cabañas*, where you make your call then pay at a desk afterwards. International calls can also be made from public telephones bearing the word *internacional*. Most are coin-operated but also take phone cards *(tarjetas tele-*

Telephones in the street are cheaper than in hotels

fónicas). For local calls, it's most convenient to buy a phone card in a tobacconist or post office, unless you have plenty of coins. If you can avoid it, don't phone from hotels, as their charges are always much higher.

The prefix for Gran Canaria is 928; for Tenerife and province, 922. For local calls the 928 is dialled as part of the number. To call other countries, dial the international access code 00, then the country code: Australia: 61, UK: 44, US & Canada: 1.

If using a US credit phone card, dial the company's access number: Sprint, tel: 900 99 00 13; AT&T, tel: 900 99 00 11; MCI, tel: 900 99 00 14.

TIME
As the Canary Islands use GMT there is no time difference from the UK. Summer Time (GMT + 1) also applies during the summer months.

ELECTRICITY
The voltage is 220v so US appliances need a transformer. Plugs are two-point, so adapters will be necessary for UK appliances.

CLOTHING
Take with you the type of clothing you would wear at home during the summer months, although during the hottest

> ### Staying healthy
> Apart from too much alcohol, the main health problems experienced by foreign visitors are upset stomachs and the effects of too much sun. The former can't be avoided entirely, but it helps to remember not to drink tap water and not to have ice in drinks, except in places where you can be pretty sure it is made with bottled water. To avoid sunstroke and sunburn, try to keep out of the midday sun, always wear sun screen and a hat, and keep children covered up as much as possible.

months (July and August) only very light clothes will be needed. Don't forget suntan lotion with a high protection factor, and a sunhat.

If you plan to walk along the beach, you will need sandals because of the heat of the sand. A sweatshirt, anorak and walking boots will be useful for mountain walks as sudden changes in the weather are commonplace. If you visit Gran Canaria during the winter you will be glad of a sweater at night.

Bare legs and shoulders are frowned on in churches. In Playa del Inglés and Maspalomas the briefest of bikini bottoms or swimming trunks seem to pass unremarked in the street.

For elegant restaurants, a jacket for men or a formal dress for women, although not always essential, will be appropriate, as the islanders like to dress up when they go out for dinner.

PHOTOGRAPHY
There's a vast array of photographic material and equipment available and prices are around the same as in the rest of Europe. Las Palmas and many tourist centres have overnight development services too – look for signs saying *Revelado en 24 horas.*

NEWSPAPERS
Gran Canaria has two newspapers – *Canarias7* and *La Provincia*. The *Canary Island Gazette* has a helpful 'What's On' section. Local news and events are also listed in *Info Canarias*. Major European dailies are on sale the same day or the day after publication in the tourist centres and Las Palmas.

MEDICAL ASSISTANCE
It is advisable to take out insurance for private treatment in the case of illness or accident. In theory, form E111 from the Department of Health (pick one up at a post office before you go), entitles UK and other EU visitors to reciprocal

medical treatment in Spain, but the procedure is rather complicated and does not cover all eventualities. The document must be presented at the Spanish Social Insurance department (Instituto Nacional de la Seguridad Social) in Las Palmas (Avenida Mesa y López, tel: 928 272 825) or in Maspalomas (Cruz de Tablero, tel: 928 142 078) in order to obtain a Spanish entitlement certificate. This must then be presented to an approved doctor.

As a rule, it is much easier to see a doctor privately for treatment, to pay for his or her services and to claim reimbursement when you get home.

Farmacias (recognisable by a large green cross outside) stock all the medicines available elsewhere in Europe, often at a lower price. They also sell some medicines over the counter that are only available on prescription in the UK. As the brand names are not always identical, go to one of the larger establishments, where the different brand names are listed on a data base.

Pharmacies are very efficient and helpful and should be the first port of call for minor complaints. There is a rota of late night chemists displayed in pharmacy windows. They are also listed in *La Provincia* newspaper.

You are unlikely to encounter language problems when seeking a doctor or a chemist in the main tourist centres, since English is widely spoken. Hotels keep lists of English-speaking doctors in the vicinity.

The following Las Palmas hospitals have emergency services *(Urgencias)*: Hospital Insular, Plaza Dr Pasteur, tel: 928 444 000; Clínica de Urgencias, León y Castillo 407, tel: 928 263 208. Inter Clinic, Sagasta 62, tel: 928 278 826, offers 24-hour access to doctors, dentists and X-rays, and specialises in treating European nationals with medical travel insurance.

In the south, there are private clinics in all the resorts; the Scandinavian Clinic, Avenida Gran Canaria 30, Playa del Inglés, tel: 928 771 538, has a good reputation.

CRIME

Crime is not a huge problem on Gran Canaria, but it is a contentious subject. Officials tend to play it down, while the press exaggerates it. You must be wary of pickpockets in the Parque Santa Catalina in Las Palmas and beach bandits in Maspalomas, and remember that markets always invite opportunistic thieves. Valuables and documents should be placed in the hotel safe for safekeeping (there are also lockers on the larger beaches). Carry photocopies of documents in case you need to show your identity for any reason.

Items left in cars are an inviting target. If you are carrying anything that even looks as if it might be valuable, keep it locked in the boot.

If the worst should happen, a report issued by the police within 24 hours of the event will be required in order to substantiate an insurance claim.

EMERGENCIES

The emergency numbers are common to all the islands:
General emergencies: 112
Police: 091
Fire: 080
Medical Emergencies: 061
Red Cross (Cruz Roja): 928 222 222

DIPLOMATIC REPRESENTATION
United Kingdom
Calle Luís Morote 6
Las Palmas
Tel: 928 262 508
United States
Calle Martínez Escobar 3
Las Palmas
Tel: 928 271 259

ACCOMMODATION

The hotel register for Gran Canaria lists hundreds of hotels, in all categories, and thousands of apartment blocks and bungalow complexes. Nonetheless, in the southern resorts, searching for accommodation on the spot is not recommended as most establishments will have been booked *en bloc* by tour operators from England and Germany. In Playa del Inglés there is currently only one *pension (hostal)* and in Puerto Rico there are no hotels at present, only apartments.

If you are going as an independent traveller, it is better to book your accommodation through a travel agent before you leave home; or use agencies such as Sun Valentin, Playa del Inglés, tel: 928 762 191, fax: 928 763 285 or Astor Travel, Playa del Inglés, tel: 928 765 325, fax: 928 765 274.

Visitors travelling independently should not assume that they will find somewhere to stay in every little town in the interior or along the north coast. Teror, which is the most important place of pilgrimage on the island, currently has only one hotel; as does Gál-

Hotel Santa Catalina in Las Palmas

dar. In both cases, the hotels are on the outskirts of town.

Hotels range from three-star accommodation, where an en suite bathroom is standard, to more luxurious hotels in the five-star category. The four- and five-star ratings correspond with international norms.

Hostales are the equivalent of a *pension* or boarding house. In a two-star establishment you can expect a shower in your room; one-star accommodation will normally only have a shared shower and toilet along the corridor. Breakfast will be available in the bar across the road. The price, however, is likely to be low.

An **apartamento** is a holiday flat. They contain one, two or more rooms, plus bathroom and kitchen with cooking equipment. *Apartamentos* are awarded between one and three keys instead of stars. They are increasingly popular and provide a relatively inexpensive and comfortable alternative to hotel accommodation, particularly for families with children. They also serve as a comfortable home-from-home for the large number of Europeans who own no property here, but who choose to spend the winter on Gran Canaria.

A **studio** is a one-room apartment without a kitchen. Single rooms with cooking facilities are usually called apartments.

There are also a number of **apart-hotels**, establishments that offer both self-catering apartments and hotel rooms and service.

Turismo rural fincas are holiday homes or hotels, either in farm houses or cottages, situated in rustic settings or in old townhouses in small towns and villages. The houses, some of them very attractive, Canarian-style buildings, have all been completely renovated with the help of EU funds.

There are only two **campsites** on Gran Canaria *(see page 126)* and camping on the beaches is usually not allowed.

Visitors should note that hotel tariffs vary considerably according to season, with summer prices being lower. It is often possible to get very advantageous deals at weekends (Friday and Saturday nights) in places that cater to a majority of business clients during the week. Therefore the price ranges given can only be approximate.

HOTEL SELECTION

The following are suggestions for some of the most popular spots. They are listed, alphabetically by town, according to the following price categories, for two people sharing a double room in high season, Nov–April. Most, but not all, include breakfast: **€€€** = over 100 euros; **€€** = 50–100 euros; **€** = under 50 euros.

Agaete

Princesa Guayarmina, Los Berrazales, tel: 928 898 009, fax: 928 898 525. This old spa hotel is 8km (5 miles) east of Agaete, situated in a romantic gorge. It is an atmospheric place with a swimming pool and 27 rooms and is very popular with walkers. **€€**.

Agüimes

Casa de los Camellos, Progreso 12, tel: 928 785 003, fax: 928 785 053. One of the *turismo rural* hotels. Attractive building with a shady courtyard; 12 en suite rooms, traditionally furnished, in the centre of this small town. Restaurant and bar. **€€**.

> **Turismo rural**
> Find out more about houses and hotels in the *turismo rural* scheme from RETUR, Calle Lourdes 2, 35320 Vega de San Mateo, tel: 928 661 668, fax: 928 661 560, <www.returcanarias.com>; or from the Turismo Rural website <www.turismoruralcanarias.com>. At present there are more villas for rent than hotels. Most are concentrated in the north, east and central areas of the island, often in places of outstanding natural beauty, and usually with access to hiking and riding trails for those who want them.

Villa de Agüimes, Sol 3, tel: 928 785 003, fax: 928 785 053. Only 6 rooms all en suite, with TV and phone and comfortably furnished. House has typical Canarian balcony and is in the centre of town. Managed by same company as above (HECANSA), hence the same contact numbers. **€€**.

Arguineguín/Patalavaca

Steigenberger La Canaria, Barranco de la Verga, tel: 928 150 400, fax: 928 151 003. A luxurious place with its own sandy beach, a large garden and attractively landscaped pool. All rooms have sea views and there are plenty of sports facilities. **€€€**.

Arucas

La Hacienda del Buen Suceso, Carreterra Arucas–Bañaderos Km 1, tel: 928 622 945, fax: 928 622 942. An excellent rural hotel set in a banana plantation just outside town. Comfortably furnished rooms, shady balconies, swimming pool, steam room and jacuzzi. €€–€€€.

Gáldar

Villa Deportiva Hermanos Monzón, Escribano de Écija s/n, Barrial 35460 Gáldar, tel: 928 551 814. This unusual place is in a suburb just outside town (left off Sardina road). Modern, comfortable accommodation is combined with a smart sports centre. Large restaurant and small bar. Good fun if you don't object to school groups in the adjacent youth hostel. €€.

Las Palmas

Astoria, Fernando Guanarteme 54, tel: 928 222 750, fax: 928 272 499. Sauna, pool and squash courts. €€.
Atlanta, Alfredo L Jones 37, tel: 928 265 062, fax: 928 273 4 85. Friendly and close to the beach. €€€.
Cantur, Sagasta 28, tel: 928 273 000, fax: 928 272 373. Welcoming place, with 124 rooms, a solarium and only 30 metres from the beach. €€.
Imperial Playa, Ferreras 1, tel: 928 468 854, fax: 928 469 442. Large, imposing hotel with comfortable

---

Beware of sharks

Newly arrived visitors toying with the idea of making Gran Canaria their second home should beware of representatives of time-share organisations. They approach visitors with the proposition of introducing them to this apparently inexpensive method of acquiring a holiday home. Too late it may occur to the visitor that the interest payments on the investment alone would have financed a holiday, even without the additional charges for administration, maintenance and repairs. However, since 1997 citizens of EU countries have been protected by a right of withdrawal within 10 days, should they have second thoughts about their purchase.

---

rooms at the northern end of Playa de las Canteras. €€.
Madrid, Plazoleta de Cairasco 4, tel: 928 360 664, fax: 928 382 176. A colonial-style hotel in a pretty little square in Triana; it's full of atmosphere and much-loved, so often full, even though the amenities are a bit old-fashioned. Breakfast not included. €.
Meliá Las Palmas, Gomera 6, tel: 928 268 050, fax: 928 268 411. The largest hotel in town, with 316 rooms, situated right on the beach. Offers the standard to be expected from a five-star establishment. Large pool, cocktail bar, restaurants, disco, convention centre, garage. €€€.
Reina Isabel, Alfredo L Jones 40, tel: 928 260 100, fax: 928 274 558. Recently renovated, it has an excellent restaurant (La Parilla), a first-class location on Playa de las Canteras, a rooftop pool and a gym. €€€.
Sansofé Palace, Portugal 68, tel: 928 224 282/224 062, fax: 928 270 784. Modern, comfortable city hotel with large rooms, right on the beach. €€€.
Santa Catalina, Parque Doramas, León y Castillo 227, tel: 928 243 040, fax: 928 242 764. Founded in 1890, this is the oldest, grandest and most expensive hotel in Las Palmas. 208 rooms, furnished with antiques; casino, pool, convention rooms. This is where the Spanish royal family and other celebrities stay. €€€.
Sol Inn Bardinos, Eduardo Benot 3, tel: 928 266 100, fax: 928 229 139. This 23-storey tower block, a city landmark, has 215 functional rooms. Ask for one on an upper floor, not just for the great view, but because the journey to the rooftop swimming pool and restaurant is shorter, and the traffic noise less disturbing. €€€.

Maspalomas

Grand Hotel Residencia, Avenida del Oasis, tel: 928 723 100, fax: 928

723 108. Exclusive new hotel built in traditional style and set in a palm grove. Attractive landscaped pool plus sporting facilities and thalassotherapy centre. €€€.

IFA Faro Hotel, Plaza del Faro 1, tel: 928 142 214, fax: 928 141 940. A four-star hotel close to the beach with two swimming pools, convention rooms and a nightclub. €€€.

Maspalomas Oasis, Plaza de las Palmeras, tel: 928 141 448, fax: 928 141 192. Vies with the Santa Catalina for the title of most luxurious hotel on the island. It's a few metres from the dunes, has 332 rooms, beautiful gardens, pools, tennis courts and luxury wherever you look. €€€.

Palm Beach, Avenida del Oasis s/n, tel: 928 140 806, fax: 928 141 808. Large new hotel, with 352 rooms in a palm grove behind the beach. €€€.

Playa del Inglés

Apolo, Avenida EEUU 28, tel: 928 760 058, fax: 928 763 918. All the services expected of a four-star hotel, but a rather noisy location. €€€.

Continental, Avenida de Italia 2, tel: 928 760 033, fax: 928 771 484. Popular with families. Gardens, pool. €€.

Beach umbrellas at San Agustín

Eugenia Victoria, Avenida de Gran Canaria 26, tel: 928 762 500, fax: 928 762 260. Central location; huge dining areas; large, pleasant rooms. €€.

Las Margaritas, Avenida Gran Canaria 38, tel: 928 761 112, fax: 928 765 380. Close to busy Avenida de Tirajana, this hotel has its own nightclub and gym, and a large pool in a stunning garden. €€.

Parque Tropical, Avenida de Italia 1, tel: 928 774 012, fax: 928 768 137. Modern hotel built in the local style in a relatively quiet location. Pleasant garden and pool. €€.

Riu Don Miguel, Avenida de Tirajana 30, tel: 928 761 508, fax: 928 771 904. Functional hotel, popular with families. Tennis, billiards available. €€.

Puerto de Mogán

Club de Mar, Urb. Puerto de Mogán,tel: 928 565 066, fax: 928 565 438. Small, attractively furnished and friendly hotel right on the quayside, with apartments as well as hotel rooms. €€.

San Agustín

Gloria Palace, Las Margaritas s/n, tel: 928 768 300, fax: 928 767 929. This smart hotel has a poolside bar, tennis courts, mini-golf, a disco and thalassotherapy centre. €€€.

Meliá Tamarindos, Las Retamas 3, tel: 928 774 090, fax: 928 774 091. Ideal for surfers and high-income tourists; casino on site. **€€€**.

Santa Brígida
Hotel Escuela Santa Brígida, Real de Coello 2, Santa Brígida, tel: 928 355 300, fax: 928 355 701. One of the prestigious HECANSA chain. Top-class service, beautiful rooms, pool, gym, sauna and large restaurant. **€€€**.

APARTMENTS/BUNGALOWS
Price categories are per night for two people in high season but there are good deals to be had at other times: **€€€** = over 80 euros; **€€** = 60–80 euros; **€** = under 60 euros.

Agaete
Apartamentos El Angosto, Obispo Pildain 11, tel/fax: 928 554 192. Peaceful, rural location; 12 well-equipped apartments in pleasant gardens; pool and restaurant; sea view. **€**.

Las Palmas
Brisamar Canteras, Paseo de las Canteras 49, tel: 928 269 400, fax: 928 269 404. Right on the beach; 41 apartments; shared gardens. **€€**.

Camping

There are only two official camp sites on the island:

Camping Guantánamo, Playa del Tauro, tel: 928 562 098. Open all year round this pleasant family site is right by a pretty beach. Children's playground, supermarket, restaurants and bars. Room for 750 people.

Camping Temisas, Lomo de la Cruz (Km 34 on the road between Agüimes and San Bartolomé), tel: 928 798 149. Woodland site with a pool and bar. Fairly basic but washrooms have electricity. Also open all year. Can accommodate 50 campers.

Colón Playa, Alfredo L Jones 45, tel: 928 265 954, fax: 928 265 958 On the beach; many of the 42 studio apartments have a balcony and sea view. **€**.
Playa Dorada, Luís Morote 61, tel: 928 265 100, fax: 928 265 104. Close to the beach, 20 apartments; TV, phone, wheelchair access. **€€**.

Maspalomas
Duna Flor Maspalomas, Avenida T. Neckermann 14, tel: 928 767 675, fax: 928 769 419. 282 bungalows; tennis and squash courts; supermarket; evening entertainment. **€€€**
Maspalomas Oasis Club, Avenida Air Marín s/n, tel: 928 142 130, fax: 928 142 518. 100 bungalows; gardens; children's playground; volley ball court. **€€**.

Playa del Inglés
Broncemar, San Crisóbal de la Laguna 7, tel: 928 773 940, fax: 928 768 573. 193 apartments with good pools, tennis court, children's playground and supermarket. **€€**.
Barbados, Avenida de Tirajana 17–19, tel: 928 760 426, fax: 928 765 102. Sixty-eight apartments; pool and gardens; bar and restaurant. **€€**.

Puerto Rico
Apartamentos El Greco, Avenida Olímpicos Doreste y Molina s/n, tel: 928 560 356, fax: 928 560 037. Attractively designed, near the beach. **€€€**
Mayagüez, Avenida Lanzarote 22, tel: 928 561 611, fax: 928 561 718. Small – 9 apartments – close to sea on Puerto Nuevo side; gardens and pool. **€**

San Agustín
IFA Interclub Atlantic, Los Jazmines 2, tel: 928 770 200, fax: 928 760 974. The biggest complex and the most expensive; multi-purpose sports court; children's playground and crèche. **€€€**

✳ INSIGHT COMPACT GUIDES

Great Little Guides to the following destinations:

Algarve	Finland	Rhodes	Jersey
Amsterdam	Florence	Rio de Janeiro	Lake District
Antigua/Barbuda	French Riviera	Rome	London
Athens	Goa	St. Lucia	New Forest
Bahamas	Gran Canaria	St. Petersburg	North York Moors
Bali	Greece	Salzburg	Northumbria
Bangkok	Holland	Shanghai	Oxford
Barbados	Hong Kong	Singapore	Peak District
Barcelona	Ibiza	Southern Spain	Scotland
Beijing	Iceland	Sri Lanka	Scottish
Belgium	Ireland	Switzerland	Highlands
Berlin	Israel	Sydney	Shakespeare
Bermuda	Italian Lakes	Tahiti	Country
Brittany	Italian Riviera	Tenerife	Snowdonia
Bruges	Jamaica	Thailand	South Downs
Brussels	Jerusalem	Toronto	York
Budapest	Kenya	Turkey	Yorkshire Dales
Burgundy	Laos	Turkish Coast	
California	Lisbon	Tuscany	USA regional:
Cambodia	Madeira	Venice	Boston
Cancún & the	Madrid	Vienna	Cape Cod
Yucatán	Mallorca	Vietnam	Chicago
Chile	Malta	West of Ireland	Florida
Copenhagen	Menorca		Florida Keys
Costa Brava	Milan	UK regional:	Hawaii – Maui
Costa del Sol	Montreal	Bath &	Hawaii – Oahu
Costa Rica	Morocco	Surroundings	Las Vegas
Crete	Moscow	Belfast	Los Angeles
Cuba	Munich	Cambridge &	Martha's Vineyard
Cyprus	Normandy	East Anglia	& Nantucket
Czech Republic	Norway	Cornwall	Miami
Denmark	Paris	Cotswolds	New Orleans
Dominican	Poland	Devon & Exmoor	New York
Republic	Portugal	Edinburgh	San Diego
Dublin	Prague	Glasgow	San Francisco
Egypt	Provence	Guernsey	Washington DC

Insight's checklist to meet all your travel needs:

■ *Insight Guides* provide the complete picture, with expert cultural background and stunning photography. Great for travel planning, for use on the spot, and as a souvenir. **186 titles.**

■ *Insight Museums & Galleries* guides to London, Paris, Florence and New York provide comprehensive coverage of each city's cultural temples and lesser known collections.

■ *Insight Pocket Guides* focus on the best choices for places to see and things to do, picked by our correspondents. They include large fold-out maps. **More than 130 titles.**

■ *Insight Compact Guides* are the fact-packed books to carry with you for easy reference when you're on the move in a destination. **More than 130 titles.**

■ *Insight FlexiMaps* combine clear, detailed cartography with essential information and a laminated finish that makes the maps durable and easy to fold. **133 titles.**

The world's largest collection of visual travel guides and maps

INDEX